40 Days & 40 Ways

Daily Meditations
for Lent - Year A

by Henry Wansbrough

*All booklets are published thanks to
the generous support of the members
of the Catholic Truth Society*

CATHOLIC TRUTH SOCIETY

PUBLISHERS TO THE HOLY SEE

Contents

Picture credits: Page 16: *Lament Around Dead Christ* by Bartolomeo Suardi called Bramantino, c.1498-1500. Brera Gallery, Milan, Italy. © Godong/Alamy Stock Photo. Page 144: *Resurrection icon* by Tirana, Albania. © Robertharding/Alamy Stock Photo.

All rights reserved. First published 2017 by The Incorporated Catholic Truth Society, 40-46 Harleyford Road London SE11 5AY. Tel: 020 7640 0042 Fax: 020 7640 0046. © 2017 The Incorporated Catholic Truth Society.

ISBN 978 1 78469 160 8

Introduction

During the season of Lent the Church brings before us a specially chosen series of readings of Scripture. I have long intended to write down a continuous series of reflections on these readings, but never got round to it until the Catholic Truth Society asked me to do so. I hope these reflections may be helpful as a focus for prayer and meditation during the blessed season of Lent. For each day I have added a possible suggestion for sanctifying the day in action.

I would suggest that the best way to use this book is to set aside some time each day during Lent. Start by reading in the Missal or Bible the two passages proposed by the Church for the Eucharist of the day. The Gospel reading is probably the more important, but the Old Testament reading will illustrate it and give it a background. Remember the old mediaeval saying, *Novum Testament in vetere latet, vetus in novo patet*, "The New Testament lies hidden in the Old, the Old lies open in the New"! Then read the reflections and finally re-read the scriptural passages, slowly and prayerfully. This should provide a fruitful basis for Lent.

Ash Wednesday

Between vestibule and altar let the priests,
the ministers of the Lord, lament. Let them say,
"spare your people, Lord!

Do not make your heritage a thing of shame,
a byword for the nations.

Why should it be said among the nations,
'Where is their God?'"

Then the Lord, jealous on behalf of his land,
took pity on his people.

Jl 2:12-18; 2 Co 5:20-6:2; Mt 6:1-6, 16-18

✠

The three readings for today send all kinds of emotions racing through the heart and the mind. They serve as a general introduction to Lent, offering for our consideration three different aspects of Lent.

First comes Joel. It is not clear what crisis is impending on Israel when Joel writes, but crisis there is, of such magnitude that bride and bridegroom must leave their chamber separately, and the priests of the Temple must beg that the people be spared. However, the Word of God is for today, not merely for the time when Joel was giving his warning. So for Christians the warning is that we are no less in crisis than those who heard the message of Joel. It is a trumpet call to change, to re-evaluate our priorities and our strivings. For us the crisis is whether I shall be ready at the end of Lent to welcome the Risen Lord as the most important person in my life. This will require some preparation!

For me the most inspiring reading for today is the second. We are to be ambassadors for Christ. As we walk around, fulfilling our daily humdrum tasks, we represent Christ to other people. As I artfully jostle just a little further in the check-out queue, as I fail to greet a lonely person in the street, am I really being an ambassador for Christ? Would I be recognised as a Christian? This is all the more important because Paul is reminding us that we have been reconciled in Christ. He does not say that we have been saved; indeed he never does - only that we *will be* saved (once that "we have been saved *in hope*") - but we have already been reconciled.

What does this mean? We were at enmity with God, a huge chasm between us. The sin of Adam, that is, the sinfulness of the whole human race, the tendency to evil, shortcomings and temptations put us on the wrong side of the chasm. When Paul says that we have already been reconciled, he must mean that the chasm is closed up. What can this mean, as I know too well that my evil tendencies still remain? It must mean that the obedience of Jesus, in his act of love for his Father on the cross, has washed away the horror and the separation of the chasm. Now I must apply this healing to myself.

The Gospel reading from Matthew is one of those lovely formulaic passages where Matthew makes his message memorable through repetition. This happens several times in the Sermon on the Mount. The formulaic framework enshrines the practice of the three good works of Judaism: prayer, fasting and almsgiving. The warning is against parading good works: they should be known only to our Father in heaven. Most of us will have digested this triple lesson, but more relevant is the insistence that what matters is the relationship between ourselves and our Father in heaven.

Action:

The purpose of Lenten resolutions is not to 'give up' or even to 'take up', but to come closer to Christ and our heavenly Father. Decide what are the sins and slacknesses which get in the way of our love of God.

Thursday after Ash Wednesday

Then to all he said, "If anyone wants to be a follower of mine, let him renounce himself and take up his cross every day and follow me. For anyone who wants to save his life will lose it; but anyone who loses his life for my sake, that man will save it."

Dt 30:15-20; Lk 9:22-25

✠

These first four days of Lent before the First Sunday of Lent set the tone in different ways. What is this butt-end of a week doing? It is a matter of counting! There should be forty days of Lent to correspond to the forty days of Jesus' time of preparation for his mission in the desert. In the Bible 'forty' is often a time of preparation: the forty years of Israel in the desert of Sinai, preparing for entry into the Promised Land, the forty days of Elijah in the desert before his vision of God, the forty days of preparation for the disciples between the Resurrection and the Ascension, preparing them for their mission. The butt-end is necessary to make up forty because Sundays, the Day of the Resurrection, can never be days of penance.

The first reading, from the Book of Deuteronomy, sets before us the stark life choice: life and prosperity or death and disaster. 'Deuteronomy' means 'Second Law', and theoretically the Book is the book found accidentally during repair of the Temple during the reforms of King Josiah. So it is a Law Book. But it is all about love, and the word 'love' occurs in it more frequently than in just about any other book of the Bible, especially focused on the loving relationship between God and the child of God - primarily Israel, but now the Church of Christ. The Law expressed the marriage contract between Israel and the Lord. Spouse must conform to spouse, and this marriage contract sets out the way Israel must behave if it is to be the loving spouse, or the loving child, of God. So the Law is itself a revelation of God's love, and observance of the Law is not so much a tiresome duty as a response in love. It is love of God which brings life and prosperity.

The other element vital to Lent which the Church sets before us today is the first prophecy of the Passion. The disciples have been drastically slow to learn who Jesus is, and at last Peter pipes up "You are the Christ" (the Anointed One, the expected Messiah). But even so, he has not appreciated what this means, for Jesus is not the expected warrior king who will sweep the Romans into the sea. His way of fulfilling the prophecies is as a suffering Messiah. So, in all the Gospels, he immediately follows the recognition of Jesus as Messiah by the first prophecy of the Passion. Each of the three great prophecies of the Passion is misunderstood by the disciples, who - like ourselves - shy away from the message that the disciple of Christ must share in his suffering. If we are to prepare to share with Christ at Easter in the Resurrection, we must do this by sharing in his suffering. Luke stresses this in today's Gospel. After the Transfiguration, as Jesus journeys up to Jerusalem, Luke gives us a series of lessons, gathered together to teach the duties and difficulties of discipleship.

Action:

Don't just stick with last year's Lenten resolutions. St Benedict suggests three things: more prayer, a regular reading of a spiritual book (this one?) and breaking a bad habit which is keeping one from God.

Friday after Ash Wednesday

Is that the sort of fast that pleases me,
a truly penitential day for men?

Hanging your head like a reed,
lying down on sackcloth and ashes?

Is that what you call fasting,
a day acceptable to the Lord?

Is 58:1-9; Mt 9:14-15

✠

The first reading, from the part of the Book of Isaiah written in Jerusalem after the return from exile in Babylon, gives a valuable lesson on fasting. It is important to get this straight at the beginning of Lent. Fasting is basically a sign of sorrow: if a loved one dies, one does not feel much like eating - though I do remember an intensely Christian couple arguing, as he lay dying, about what sort of sandwiches they should provide at his funeral. It is one element in disaster behaviour, when everything goes upside down, like tearing the clothes and throwing dust on the head. In the next stage it becomes a deliberate signal of sorrow, and so of repentance. In this capacity it is also a signal of self-denial. Isaiah's complaint is that the people of Jerusalem were using it as an artificial sign of repentance, so as a meaningless, merely external sign and so false. There was no point in fasting if it was not an expression of return to the important, real points of God's requirements, reverence for the Sabbath, social justice, care for the needy and marginalised. So our fasting and Lenten resolutions are pointless if they are not linked to and inspired by the desire to think the thoughts of God and to please God.

The Gospel reading seems at first sight a puzzling choice, for it justifies the disciples of Jesus actually refraining from fasting. The Pharisees, who observed the Law very strictly, fasted regularly, but Jesus' disciples did not. "Why not?" they ask, with the implication, "Does not every seriously religious person fast?"

Jesus then introduces the wonderful image of the wedding feast. Right the way through the Old Testament the prophets had likened the last times, when God would finally come to his people and set everything right, to a wedding feast, the completion of the wedding of God and his people. Hosea had proclaimed,

I am going to lead her out into the desert and
  speak to her heart.

There she will respond to me as she did when
  she was young,

as she did when she came out of the land of Egypt.

Now, when Jesus has come, is the time of that wedding feast, an image which Jesus uses in so many of his parables.

But wait a moment: there is something wrong. "When the bridegroom is taken away". That does not happen at a wedding feast. The bridegroom will eventually *go* away, but not *be taken*. From the very beginning of the Gospel (and in Mark this occurs in the first confrontation with the Pharisees) we are being warned that this bridegroom's path will not be smooth and comfortable.

Wedding feast it is, but a sort of suspended wedding feast, so that even after the Resurrection Christians may fast to share their Master's path.

Action:

One way of getting to know Jesus better during Lent would be to read a passage of the Gospel each day reflectively, slowly and with prayer. Mark is the shortest, and he is a splendid storyteller, with a graphic style which brings it all to life. Look out for the visual details!

Saturday after Ash Wednesday

Jesus said to them in reply, "It is not those who are well
who need the doctor, but the sick. I have not come
to call the virtuous, but sinners to repentance."

Is 58:9-14; Lk 5:27-32

✠

This preliminary week ends with further teaching from
the Old Testament and from Jesus himself about real
devotion, preparing us to see what Lent is really all about.
The first reading carries on with the same chapter of Isaiah
as yesterday, scraping through the cobwebs of automatic
observance to get to the true way of responding to God's
call. "If you banish the yoke from among you", or in other
words, if you free your neighbour from oppression, if you
do not oppress others and make them subservient to your
will. "If you do away with the pointed finger and malicious
gossip", or in other words, if you respect and honour others
rather than making fun of them and defaming them behind
their backs. "If you call the Sabbath delightful", or for us,
if we really do make Sunday a joyful day, gladly dedicated
to the Lord you will be responding to God's call.

What this really means is made clear by Jesus' shocking
statements in the Gospel. That Jesus should call a degraded

tax collector to be one of his close associates is bad enough, for tax collectors were despised and shunned on religious grounds: they worked for the unclean Romans. But that is not all! The Pharisees saw sanctity to consist in perfect, detailed observance of God's Law (and what is wrong with that?), but Jesus drove a horse and cart through that by having a merry party with dirty tax collectors and other sinners, whose company he seemed to enjoy. It is striking to see how willingly they left their lucrative, but degrading employment: here Levi; in another version of the story it is Matthew; and at Jericho the story is told of Zacchaeus. Either Jesus lost all claim to be God's representative or the Pharisees had got their priorities wrong.

So Jesus replies with two of those splendid, forceful contrasts which are so characteristic of his speech: not *healthy* but *sick*, not *virtuous* but *sinners*. In other words, it is not the details of the Law which matter, but the purpose of the Law: to bring men and women to God. We can see here the authentic words of Jesus, for he is always using such contrasts, usually with four members: "what *God* has **joined** no *human* may **separate**". These stark contrasts are always built on Scripture, too, in that case the joining of man and woman in the Creation story of Genesis. Or "*man* is not made for the **Sabbath**, but the **Sabbath** for man", again with reference to "made for" in the Creation story, all about the making of the world. As an inspired and inspiring oral teacher Jesus was master of the forceful word; it is no surprise that he unerringly penetrated directly to the meaning of Scripture, more profoundly than those who stood against him could ever hope to do.

Action:

It might be worth examining whether I keep anyone under a yoke, and just how much finger pointing and malicious gossip is part of my way of life.

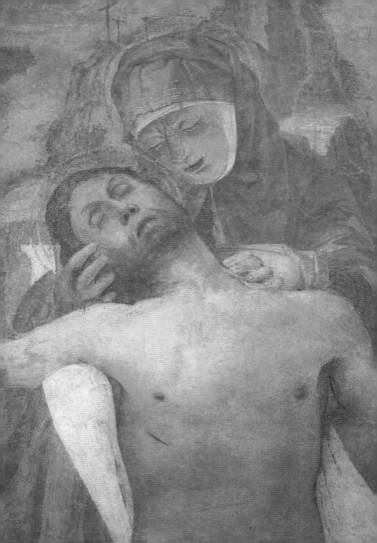

First Sunday of Lent

> *If it is certain that death reigned over everyone as the consequence of one man's fall, it is even more certain that one man, Jesus Christ, will cause everyone to reign in life who receives the free gift that he does not deserve, of being made righteous.*
>
> *Gn 2:7-9; 3:1-7; Rm 5:12-19; Mt 4:1-11*

✠

Note: Reflections on the Gospel readings for the Sundays of Lent are available in the CTS booklet 'Companion to the Sunday Gospels Year A'. Here we will therefore concentrate on the first two readings for the Sundays.

The story of the Fall of Adam and Eve is only too familiar - in ourselves. The story is not, of course, even meant to be historical, a story of what happened some millions of years ago when humans first came into being. When humans first became capable of moral (and so immoral) action they were far too primitive for such a gem of a story. Furthermore, the Bible teaches by many other forms of writing than history. Many of the books of the Bible (for instance Job, Jonah and Judith) are sheer fiction, but still teach us an important lesson from the Lord. This story is far more important than a mere account of the past: it is an analysis of human behaviour. The Hebrew word 'adam' means 'human being'; it seems to be an individual name, but in fact is the name of our whole species. This splendid human couple, representative of the whole human race, made in the image of God to populate the world, knows well what God requires of them, but fails to keep to the high principles. Overcome by self-interest, and pride in their own ability to decide what is best for themselves, they descend into the misery of failure and shame. But God still does not desert them, but comes looking for them in their distress, and covers their shame by sewing them the first clothes. Divine love is not easily deflected.

Nor is the calm and peace of the Garden of Eden necessarily in the past. It is a representation of how the world should be, of what is spoilt by the disharmony of human failure. It is the harmony, human and ecological, for which we long and strive, to be perfected in the renewal of the world in the last days. Our hope is to emerge from this state of disharmony into the peace of God's Kingdom.

Paul's Letter to the Romans gives the other side of the picture: "If death came to many through the offence of one man, how much more plentiful has been the grace of God and the free gift in the love of the one man Jesus Christ, coming to so many!" To Paul, thinking in Hebrew, the word 'man' in this quotation would be 'adam'. So Paul looks at the Adam story as though it were history (the literary studies which enable us to see the true genre of the writing were still long in the future!), but he also sees Christ as the Second Adam, a reflection of the First Adam, corresponding to the First Adam, but reversing the disaster. The central idea is that Christ's obedience to the Father undid or wiped away the disobedience of the First Adam. It was not the bloodiness of the sacrifice or the pain, but the loving obedience of Jesus that forms the central point.

Action:

The Lord's Day is a day of joy, not fasting. Bring some real joy to the members of your family!

Monday

"When the Son of Man comes in his glory, escorted by all the angels, then he will take his seat on his throne of glory.
All the nations will be assembled before him and he will separate men one from another as the shepherd separates sheep from goats."

Lv 19:1-2, 11-18; Mt 25:31-46

✠

The first reading, from Leviticus, perhaps the most detailed Book of the Law, gives us a series of commands about living in community and how to treat other members of the community. Many of them occur also in the law codes of surrounding peoples of the Ancient Near East of the time of Moses, many of them also in modern law codes. Human nature, with its needs and temptations, remains roughly the same from age to age. Perhaps there are variations of application for an agrarian, a mechanised and an electronic age. This law code has two important differences from the codes of surrounding lands. First, it stresses that all human beings have the same dignity: there is the same penalty for wounding a slave as for wounding a free person, whereas in other codes the status of the wounded person determines the penalty: a nobleman is more valuable than a slave. Second, it is more human, more interior, leaving room for feelings and intentions: so the command is to settle a quarrel frankly, not to bear a grudge, not to exact vengeance.

But the most important difference is that in the Hebrew version the Lord is seen as the source and guarantor of the legislation. It is not just human legislation, but prescriptions for the children of God. "Be holy as I am holy" is the refrain of this part of the Book, and by obeying these Laws the Israelite in some way partakes of the holiness of God. What is holiness? It is being associated with the Lord, set apart from ordinary life, somehow by delegation sharing in God's own powers, and above all set apart as 'special' and even awesome.

As for the parable of the Sheep and Goats, it is in many ways the climax of Matthew's teaching. It comes at the end, so as the conclusion, of the last of his five discourses, five gatherings of Jesus' teaching on different subjects. After the teaching in Matthew 24 on the final coming of the Son of Man, Matthew gives two pairs of parables about being ready for this coming, (the Burglar and the Conscientious Steward, the Ten Wedding Attendants and the Ten Talents). The whole then concludes with the Sheep and the Goats. All these parables are typical of Matthew, contrast parables in which good and bad are sharply contrasted - not like Luke's parables, in which the reader has a sneaking sympathy for the Prodigal Son and the Crafty Steward. Matthew's characters are entirely good or entirely bad, unlike Luke's who often do the right thing for the wrong reason!

Two other remarkable features: only here in the Gospel do we see the Son of Man seated on his throne as king and surrounded by his (not God's) angels; it is Jesus who declares the final judgement of God, so the climax of Matthew's Christology. Second, the judgement is based not on faith (as in Paul) or on love (as in John), but entirely on the good works done for the sake of Christ: "in so far as you did this to one of the least of these brothers or sisters of mine, you did it to me".

Action:

The most valuable thing most people have to give is time. What about visiting a sick friend or relative? Or even someone who has no relatives to cheer them?

Tuesday

*Jesus said to his disciples: "In your prayers do not
babble as the pagans do, for they think that by using
many words they will make themselves heard.
Do not be like them; your Father knows what you
need before you ask him."*

Is 55:10-11; Mt 6:7-15

✠

The principal reading for today is undoubtedly the
Lord's Prayer. Matthew puts this right in the middle of
the Sermon on the Mount, interrupting his long passage
(Ash Wednesday's Gospel) on doing good works in secret.
Since the Sermon on the Mount is Matthew's gathering of
Jesus' teaching on conditions for entering the Kingdom of
Heaven, one could say that he deliberately puts this in the
very centre of the conditions.

The Lord's Prayer exists in several slightly different
versions, not only in Matthew, Luke and an ancient,
perhaps first-century, Christian document, *The Didache*,
but also somewhat more differently among Jewish prayers.
The prayer begins with an invocation, and then divides into
two halves, each of three requests, the first three regarding
God, the second three regarding Christian disciples. The

invocation differs in Matthew "Our Father in heaven") and Luke (simply "Father"). The latter has a lovely warmth and simplicity, like Jesus' prayer, "Abba, Father" in Gethsemane. "Abba" is not, as some have thought, a kiddies' word like "Daddy", but is the warm and respectful greeting from an adult member of the family. Perhaps Matthew added "Our" to make it a community prayer, and "in heaven" to avoid confusion with an earthly father.

The three different petitions about God are really variants of the same prayer. The central petition, "may your kingship come", is a prayer for the completion of God's plan, may the Kingship of God be fulfilled, an eschatological yearning that God's sovereignty over the world be totally accepted and unimpeded. The Pharisees thought this would be the case when the Law was perfectly obeyed. Christians might well agree, though with a different interpretation of what this obedience would be. The first petition, "may your name be held holy", is similar, a prayer that the sacred, unpronounceable Name, the Lord, may be honoured and revered as it should be. It is the way Ezekiel 36:20-23 describes the complete vindication of God's name and honour at the re-establishment of God's people in a free Jerusalem. It never really occurred at the return from Exile, for Jerusalem continued to be harassed and dominated by foreign powers. The third petition (not given by Luke) is a typically Matthaean formula; he often stresses that it is not enough to cry "Lord, Lord" without actually doing the will of the Father. It also forms Jesus' second, heartfelt prayer in Gethsemane, "may your will be done".

Then we turn to human needs. First, to keep us fed - not just on bread, for the Hebrew word for bread is often used more widely for food in general. Second, that dangerous prayer for forgiveness on condition that we forgive others - a petition which must always be accompanied with searching our own consciousness for forgiveness of others. This again is the central petition of the three, and is further stressed by Matthew by repetition at the end of the prayer, and by the parable of the Unforgiving Debtor. Finally, the two complementary prayers, "lead us not into trials" and "deliver us from evil" - this may be understood either of the abstract entity "evil" or the personification of evil, "the Evil One".

Action:

Take each of these petitions and savour it separately for a few minutes. Which best fits your own prayer and conception of our relationship with God?

Wednesday

> *"This is a wicked generation; it is asking for a sign.*
> *The only sign it will be given is the sign of Jonah.*
> *For just as Jonah became a sign to the Ninevites,*
> *so will the Son of Man be to this generation."*
>
> *Jon* 3:1-10; *Lk* 11:29-32

✠

It must be admitted that the first reading from Jonah is put in only to support and explain the reference in the Gospel reading, but I refuse to let Jonah slip out of sight like that! It is a delightful Book, a sort of joke, and certainly a satire. It is fiction, with no historical basis at all, but it teaches an important lesson, both to the original hearers and to ourselves. The story goes like this:

Jonah the prophet is given the task of preaching to the great city of Nineveh, telling them that they are to be destroyed for their wickedness. He baulks at this task and attempt to evade it by taking a ship in the opposite direction. God will have none of this, has him shipwrecked, swallowed by a great fish and vomited up on the shore. Thereupon God repeats the order, and this time Jonah obeys. He goes to Nineveh and preaches, at which the whole city from the king downwards puts on sackcloth and fasts (even the animals!) in repentance. Finding that they are not to be destroyed, Jonah is furious with God and reckons that God has made a fool of him; he doesn't care that thousands of Ninevites have been saved.

The lesson is that the chosen prophet of the Chosen People directly disobeys God, while by contrast the wicked pagan city immediately responds to the call for repentance. So don't think that you can be complacent just because you belong to the Chosen People. Outright pagans can be better than the Chosen People. The message of course is also relevant to Christians!

The story of Jonah is linked to the Gospel reading in two ways: resurrection and repentance. We need to be reminded periodically as we go through Lent that we are heading for the Resurrection of Jesus. The sign of the prophet Jonah is the three days he spent inside the big fish (often called a whale, though the whale is a mammal, not a fish!) In Mark's version of this saying (*Mk* 8:12) Jesus says he will give no sign. Running through the Gospels is a theme of the refusal of a sign. Presumably some of Jesus' hearers were expecting a staggering sign which would leave no possibility of failure to be convinced. This is not offered to us, for the acceptance of Jesus and of faith is always an act of free will; we are not bludgeoned into faith! The Resurrection of Jesus is of course a wonder far beyond any powers of nature, but it is not a staggering public miracle, and still needs faith for its understanding. When Jesus says he will give a sign like the sign of the prophet Jonah he is referring to the symbolic meaning of the three days hidden away.

There is also the link that Jonah preached repentance, as did Jesus himself; some responded, some not. A difference is that Jesus proclaimed the Good News before his three days in the tomb, not afterwards, as Jonah. This is a reminder that we are the ones who now proclaim the Good News.

Action:

Is there anyone unhappy or bereaved in the neighbourhood, to whom I could bring happiness by a visit?

Thursday

*Jesus said to his disciples; "Ask, and it will be given
to you; search, and you will find; knock, and the door
will be opened to you. For the one who asks always
receives; the one who searches always finds; the one
who knocks will always have the door opened to him."*

Est 4:17; Mt 7:7-12

✠

The reading from Esther is one of only two readings from
this Book in the Lectionary - the other being a long prayer
of praise. Both of them are taken from the Greek version of
the Book, which adds several prayers to the Hebrew text.
It is a fictional story, placed in the Exile, about a Hebrew
Queen of Persia, who saves herself and her race by her piety
and fidelity to the Law. It has the charm and the 'Arabian
Nights' atmosphere of the legendary royal courts of the
East - as well as a fairly bloody ending - but the prayers
are delicate and heartfelt. Today it is included to pair with
the reading from Matthew about earnest petitionary prayer.

Petitionary prayer is certainly a problem theologically.
We address our prayers to God as a child would persuade a
parent, begging to be allowed some indulgence, "Mummy,
may I stay up late to watch Ding the Dong?" Do I really

think that God is going to change the course of the world, put the normal causes into reverse, at my prayers? What if I am praying for fine weather at the seaside while a farmer is praying for rain to raise his crops? Two opposing sides praying for victory in a sports fixture? Does the most fervent side win? God cannot please both of us. Nor can you escape the dilemma by timing. "God knew all the time that I was going to pray in this way at this particular moment, and will have arranged the world accordingly. He knew that my prayer would be the most fervent. Anyway, God knows everything, so knows what I want. Is there any point in telling him about it?"

Is it merely an expression of trust and affection, in the same way that we tell those we love that we love them, though they know it well already? Certainly every prayer includes a sort of subtext of trust in God as Father. Certainly (like begging children) we try to behave a little better, so that we may deserve the prayer to be granted. Part of our prayer is to tell our Father that we trust him, and trust that he will do whatever is best for us and for others. So the subtext always includes, though perhaps rather grudgingly, "thy will be done on earth as in heaven". We do pray that our prayer may be granted, but at the same time we pray that we may have the trust in God to accept whatever he sends us, granting that we may not know what is best for us in these particular circumstances.

The reading ends with the Golden Rule, which occurs not only in Christianity and Judaism, but in many other religions also. It often comes in negative form, "Do not do to others what you do not want done to yourself", but here it is given in the more challenging, positive form. The Christian must leave his or her comfort zone and take positive action.

Action:

Pray a couple of decades of the Rosary for someone else's intentions - or even take up the habit of praying the Rosary each day.

Friday

*So then, if you are bringing your offering to the altar
and there remember that your brother has something
against you, leave your offering there before the altar,
go and be reconciled with your brother first, and then
come back and present your offering.*

Ez 18:21-28; Mt 5:20-26

✠

Today's two readings are all about repentance and conversion
from sin. The first reading, from Ezekiel, is to be seen against
the background of the Babylonian Exile. In the second
generation of the Exile the exiles from Judah will have been
wondering why they should suffer for the sins of their fathers
and other ancestors. Judah was sent into exile by the Lord
because of its persistent failure to keep the Law or to put
their trust in the Lord. There had been a series of reforms,
but none of them lasted long before idolatry broke out again
and even such horrors as the sacrifice of children to Baal
or Moloch. When threatened with attack from the outside,
instead of turning to the Lord, they had appealed to Egypt,
that broken reed. There was corporate corruption, followed
by the disaster of the Exile to Babylon, in which they lost
Temple, sacrifice, King and city - everything they held dear.

But the disaster turned into a blessing because religion became a much more personal commitment, no longer a national bond to a national God, but a personal bond of personal loyalty. Such is the context of the present reading: each person is responsible for personal sins and none others, is to be punished for them and no others, and to be rewarded for personal loyalty and personal conversion. The responsibility is no longer on the clan, but on the individual, and conversion - in either direction - redounds on the individual.

This is obviously true and important, but the Christian is also aware that personal sins and personal fidelity affect the whole Body of Christ. If I live among gangsters and drunkards I will more easily slip into their standards of behaviour. If I live among saints I should be drawn up to follow their example and share in their sanctity.

The Gospel reading is drawn from the first 'working' section of the Sermon on the Mount, just after the initial proclamation of the Beatitudes. There follow six ways in which Jesus' teaching goes beyond that of the Old Testament (and consequently of the Pharisees and their scribes, or lawyers). The first and last of these are about love and the practice of love. This first contrast is about the opposite of love, namely enmity. Enmity to a brother or sister creates such a painful wound in the Body of Christ that it rules out sacrifice and prayer. We must leave our sacrifice at the altar and go and be reconciled with our brother or sister. This is the importance of the exchange of greetings at the Sign of Peace in the Eucharist. The peace filters down, hand to hand, from Christ at the altar to the whole congregation. In the present state of Church going it is, of course, important to remember also those members who are not physically present.

Action:

Is there any broken relationship which needs mending? A properly healed relationship should be stronger and warmer than the original friendship.

Saturday

Jesus said to his disciples: "You have learnt how it was said: You must love your neighbour and hate your enemy. But I say this to you: love your enemies and pray for those who persecute you; in this way you will be sons of your Father in heaven".

Dt 26:16-19; Mt 5:43-48

✠

There are, of course, a lot of laws in Deuteronomy ('the Second Law'), but as soon as the heading 'Deuteronomy' appears one can expect also some expression of a loving relationship to God, but only 'if you follow his ways'. You cannot love someone while continuing to behave in ways which that person finds unpalatable or unacceptable. Today's passage begins the conclusion of the Book which sums it up. The promise to be God's very own special people conveys a very special affection, as though God was clasping us in his arms. But he can't clasp someone who is wriggling to get away the whole time.

The promise of Deuteronomy today leads on to the last of the six contrasts in the Sermon on the Mount, the first of which was given to us yesterday. Just like the first, this too is about love. Nowhere in the Scripture does it say 'you must hate your enemy', but Jesus was given to making his point by means of emphatic contrasts, and it should perhaps be understood less sharply than its face value. In the same way he says that no one can be his disciple without hating father and mother (*Lk* 14:26), which surely is to be understood as putting Christ before father and mother - if such a dreadful decision should occur - rather than as positively hating them. In any case, here Jesus is teaching that we must love all people unreservedly. The Old Testament Law in Leviticus 19:18 had prescribed to love your neighbour as yourself. The word there used for 'neighbour' widens family love to include the whole People of God, but does not go beyond that. Here Jesus widens it further, to all the recipients of the Father's rain, good and bad, honest and dishonest, so beyond the confines of the Chosen People. More sharply still, it flies in the face of all natural reciprocal relationships by laying down love of enemies. The Christian must make a point of initiating the breakdown of any enmity.

There are two further dimensions to this series of six corrections of the Mosaic Law. First, by putting unlimited love at the beginning and end of the series Matthew (and surely we must assume that Matthew in his Sermon on the Mount is the editor of Jesus' thoughts) forms a sort of bracket which implies that love is the theme and common factor of all six corrections. Second, the series ends with the staggering demand, "you must be perfect as your heavenly Father is perfect". Luke, in his corresponding passage, applies this more narrowly: "Be merciful as your Father is merciful" (6:36). A similar demand is made only once in the whole of the Gospels, to the rich young man in Matthew 21:19, "if you will be perfect..." How absolute this requirement of love is, however, is made plain at the cross, where Jesus' final word is "It is perfected/consummated" (*Jn* 19:30).

Action:

Bring peace and love into some situation where there is no peace and love. This will need careful thought and no little tact!

Second Sunday of Lent

*This grace had already been granted to us, in Christ
Jesus, before the beginning of time, but it has only
been revealed by the Appearing of our saviour Christ
Jesus. He abolished death, and he has proclaimed life
and immortality through the Good News.*

Gn 12:1-4a; 2 *Tm* 1:8-10; *Mt* 17:1-9

✠

Again, we will concentrate on the first two readings, as a
reflection on the Gospel reading is available in *Companion
to the Sunday Gospels Year A*, also published by CTS.
Today is the Sunday of the Transfiguration.

The first readings of Sundays are normally paired with
the Gospel readings to help illustrate the lesson of the
reading. However, during Lent they form an independent
series, different in Years A, B and C. In each yearly cycle
the readings work through the history of the Chosen
People from Adam (last week) to the promise of the New
Covenant (fifth Sunday), which is to be fulfilled at Easter.
So now we start the story of the Chosen People with the
Call of Abraham.

It is a mysterious call. We are not told how it happened; was it a voice? Was it an unseen presence? Was it just an inexplicable experience? God makes himself known in mysterious ways, even today. Abraham did not know, and was not told, that God was Creator of the universe; this was probably a thought which would have been too great for Abraham to comprehend. He did not know that God was transcendent or invisible or omnipotent or everywhere. We do not know even that he knew the story of Adam. All he knew was that this presence had promised to be his protector, and he trusted that protector, threw over everything he had, and went out into the desert without even a son for his old age.

God's blessing can be read to mean either "All tribes of the earth will bless themselves by you" or "...will use your name as a blessing". In either case the call of Abraham which initiated the vocation of the Hebrews or Israelites is a blessing not only for Israel, but for the whole world. The vocation of Israel was not narrow; it was to bring salvation to the whole world - as became clearer and clearer in the course of the revelation in the Old Testament, until it was realised and completed in Christ's death and Resurrection.

The Second Letter to Timothy seems to have been written by Paul as an old man, a prisoner and awaiting the release of death. It is a valedictory letter, a sort of last will and testament of the apostle. He has been through a hard time for the sake of the Good News, and knows that he has been sanctified by this experience. Now, as we in Lent are looking forward to Easter, he is looking forward to the appearance of Christ. This term, also translated, the 'Epiphany' or 'Manifestation', occurs only in the final Pauline letters. Its meaning seems to hover between the great final manifestation of Christ at the end of time and the awesome meeting with Christ which awaits each of us at death. In either case, for every Christian it is the moment of final consummation.

Action:

Invite a lonely person to some pleasant and comforting shared experience.

Monday

*Jesus said to his disciples: "Be compassionate as your
Father is compassionate."*

Dn 9:4-10; Lk 6:36-38

✠

The atmosphere of the day is given by the first sentence
of the Gospel reading. Matthew ends the first section of
his Sermon on the Mount with the command to be perfect
as our heavenly Father is perfect, as we heard a couple
of days ago. As might be expected from Matthew, who
thinks in Jewish terms of the fulfilment of the Law, this
presupposes that there is a sort of blueprint of perfection,
outlined in perfect obedience to God's commands. Luke's
formulation of this saying of Jesus is more fluid, formed in
terms of a generous and open welcome, "Be compassionate
as your Father is compassionate." This is filled out in the
sentences which follow: we may not judge others, but must
give an open pardon if we wish to avoid a strict judgement
ourselves according to our deserts.

The first reading from Daniel (a Book written at the
time of the Maccabean Revolt in 176 BC) shows that in
the time after the return from the Exile there was in Israel
a vivid awareness of guilt, a tender consciousness and

a sense of shame for the sins of the ancestors which led
to the Exile. This is expressed in many of the writings
of the time, but none more insistently than the Book of
Baruch. For Christians this awareness of guilt is part of the
preparation for the coming of Christ, an awareness of the
rotten condition from which we were to be redeemed by
Christ: the basis of all Israel's relationship to God. From
the very first God is not content to leave the human race
wallowing in guilt. So in the story of the Fall, God comes
to search for the human couple, hiding their nakedness
(their shame and vulnerability) in the Garden, and actually
sews them garments to hide their shame and assuage their
vulnerability. When God reveals to Moses his sacred Name
YHWH, he does not tell Moses its meaning; only after
Israel has sinned by worshipping the golden bull (called a
"golden calf" to demean it!) does God reveal the meaning:
he passes before Moses, crying "the Lord, the Lord, God
of tenderness and mercy, slow to anger, rich in kindness
and faithfulness, forgiving faults, transgressions, sin" (*Ex*
34:6). This self-definition of the Name is the title which
echoes down the Scripture, recurring again and again. It is,
so to speak, central to the being of God to forgive.

For us forgiveness is one of the hardest things in the
world. Note how often in the Bible God cements his
forgiveness by giving an extra present (the clothes in the
story of the Fall)! Just so, a mother forgiving a child may

cement the forgiveness by a little present to wipe out the shame and disquiet and show the restoration of real love. Not a bad idea!

Action:

Give a small token of affection, to cultivate and nourish the love with someone we have recently forgiven.

Tuesday

*You, however, must not allow yourselves to be called
Rabbi, since you have only one Master, and you are all
brothers. You must call no one on earth your father,
since you have only one Father, and he is in heaven.*

Is 1:10, 16-20; *Mt* 23:1-12

✠

The first reading sets the scene. It is the first public
proclamation in the Book of Isaiah. The Book is not of
course a straight, chronological run through of the sayings
of one prophet, but is a collection of sayings. Put first
in the Book is the invitation to the rulers of Jerusalem -
addressing them as the rulers of those cities, Sodom and
Gomorrah, the very archetypes of wickedness - to repent.
This is always a principal theme for us in Lent.

The Gospel reading is in the same vein, an excerpt
from Matthew 23, the chapter containing a seven-fold
condemnation (seven is the perfect number, so a total
condemnation), lashing the Pharisees and their scribes.
In the Christian world the name 'Pharisee' has become
identical with 'hypocrite'. By the time the Gospels were
formed and written down the Pharisees were the only
stream of Judaism still in existence. Sadducees, centred on

the Temple, had been wiped out in the destruction of the Temple, and Essenes (at least in their settlement on the shore of the Dead Sea) also. The Pharisees were therefore the mainspring of Jewish opposition to the followers of Jesus, and this later hostility was read into the earlier historical situation.

At the centre of this later opposition would have been not the recognition of Jesus as Messiah or Christ, but the refusal of Christians to continue to observe the Jewish law, whereas the very first Christians retained at least elements of Jewish legal observance. Right conduct, observance of the Law, was much more important than the details of belief. Where there is stress on exact observance of the details of law there is always an opening for accusations of hypocrisy. Witness the timing of the Eucharistic fast: the timing of when I eat my last mouthful can be more important than the purpose of interior preparation to welcome the Lord. The importance of practices can easily become more absorbing than their intended purpose.

There is even a possibility that Jesus himself was a marginal Pharisee. The Pharisees took no part in the condemnation and death of Jesus; they are simply not there in the narrative. His opponents in Jerusalem were the Sadducees, who were in charge of Jerusalem. Argument about legal observance is part of the Jewish way of life, even today, and the controversies in the story of Jesus could well have been in-house discussions about the interpretation of the Law, rather than hostile confrontations. He even used - and used brilliantly - the Pharisaic method of quoting the Law in argument, setting text against text, and the recognised rules of interpretation. Perhaps the chief oddity of his interpretation (from the Pharisaic point of view) was to put the Law of love of neighbour on a level with love of God.

Action:

Gather together some superfluous clothes/books etc. and think of who could benefit from them.

Wednesday

No; anyone who wants to be great among you must be
your servant, and anyone who wants to be first among
you must be your slave, just as the Son of Man came
not to be served but to serve, and to give his life as
a ransom for many.

Jr 18:18-20; Mt 20:17-28

✠

The reading from Jeremiah draws attention to the close parallel between Jeremiah and Jesus, for Jeremiah was heavily persecuted and almost killed for proclaiming the message he was given, persecuted for trying to help his countrymen by drawing them back to fidelity to the Law. He tried to evade the call at first, by pretending to God that he had a stammer and could not speak properly. His prophecy is interrupted by several passages which show how tough he found this ministry, when he turns to God in his distress, begging to be relieved of his task.

In the Gospel reading the third of Jesus' great prophecies of the Passion is immediately followed by the request of the mother of Zebedee's sons for a high position in the Kingdom. She has simply not listened to the words of the Master. In Mark's Gospel (the earliest Gospel, which

Matthew knew and used) it is worse, for there the request is made by the sons of Zebedee themselves directly after hearing what is to befall Jesus. Obviously Matthew wanted to tone down the rebuke and criticism of the disciples who are to become the leaders of the Church. In Mark they are several times sharply criticised for their slowness in understanding who Jesus is, and, still more, for their failure to understand that the follower of Jesus must take up his cross and follow to suffering and death.

Then, just as yesterday's Gospel outlawed titles of honour like 'Rabbi' and 'Father', so now today's passage underlines that the only dignity in the Christian Church is service. Ministry of priest or bishop is not a dignity, but a service, for the Son of Man came not to be served but to serve, and priest and bishop and others participate in this same ministry of service. The titles of honour, 'My Lord', 'Your Eminence', etc., have no validity in the Church except in so far as they indicate a sharing in Christ's ministry of service.

The title which Jesus here calls himself, 'Son of man', is a mysterious title. In the Book of Ezekiel the prophet is so addressed by the angelic interpreter of his visions. It there means 'human being'. In Aramaic at the time of Jesus it seems to be used also to mean 'a human person', but often in the sense in which 'one' is used in English, a delicate self-allusion ('one may think', 'one finds that...').

Jesus uses it to avoid shocking when speaking about his suffering, or to avoid boasting when speaking about his authority. But it also seems to allude to the Son of Man in Daniel's prophecy (*Dn* 7:13), who comes to the One of Great Age and receives from him all authority on earth. This makes it a low-key, but staggering claim to limitless, indeed superhuman, authority, the most awesome of any description of Jesus, especially when Jesus says to the High Priest, "You will see the Son of Man seated at the right hand of the Power and coming on the clouds of heaven" (*Mt* 26:64).

Action:

Spend a few minutes in prayer, perhaps before the Blessed Sacrament, to meditate on the awesome greatness of Jesus, the Son of Man.

Thursday

There was a rich man who used to dress in purple and fine linen and feast magnificently every day. And at his gate there lay a poor man called Lazarus, covered with sores, who longed to fill himself with the scraps that fell from the rich man's table. Dogs even came and licked his sores.

Jr 17:5-10; Lk 16:19-31

✠

The reading from Jeremiah prepares for the Gospel contrast between the two destinations of the rich man and Lazarus. The same contrast is used in Psalm 1, put at the head of the psalter. Its imagery also brings vividly to life the stark contrasts of the Holy Land, the dauntingly arid desert of Judaea and the green fruitfulness of the hill country. I once had to give a ten-minute lecture in Hebrew as part of a language course in Jerusalem, and took as my theme, "Why did God choose Israel?" Answer: "Because life there is so obviously dependent on God's gift of climate and rain." "No", said the teacher surprisingly, "it is because Jerusalem is the centre of the earth!"

The parable of the Rich Man and Lazarus perhaps functions as Luke's equivalent to Matthew's final parable of the Sheep and Goats, with the same lesson, that our final reward or failure depends on our treatment of those in need - any kind of need, spiritual and emotional as well as material and financial. But the poor are of particular concern to Luke. He moves in a richer world: his vocabulary is more sophisticated. It is no longer Mark's peasant or cornershop world of barter and borrowing, but a more developed, supermarket (almost shopping mall) world of larger sums of money, of bankers and rates of interest. In this richer world there is all the more need to stress a duty to the poor: Luke's Beatitudes are not on "the poor in spirit" but "the poor", not "those who hunger and thirst for justice" but simply "those who hunger and thirst", who don't know where their next meal is coming from.

It is typically Lukan. Luke conjures up a scene in a few words, the sumptuous rich man's banquet, with its purple and tablecloth, and the squalor of Lazarus. The dogs licking his sores are not charming sympathisers, but squalid, flea-ridden curs. There are no pet animals in that world: dogs are either fierce guard dogs or mangy beggars, and the sore licking is meant to evoke disgust. Whereas in Matthew the characters are absolute, totally good or totally bad, in Luke we have a sneaking liking for the anti-hero, who does at least show affection and care for his unreformed brothers! In the same way the Prodigal Son does win our sympathy, and the Unjust Judge, although their motives for doing the right thing are not too bright. And how Luke's characters chatter! Luke loves to report direct speech, even though Abraham and the rich man have to bawl to each other across the unbridgeable chasm: in the same way in the parable of the Great Supper for Matthew the unwilling invited guests simply turn away in grim silence, while in Luke's version they scrape up and tell their improbable excuses about buying a new yacht or new combine harvester (or whatever).

The final paragraph brings us also into the post-Resurrection world: even when the Resurrection has actually happened people will refuse to believe.

Action:

If you have something to give, give something. If nothing, a genuine greeting to the vendor of The Big Issue on the street corner or the struggling mother may remind them that there are people who care.

Friday

*Listen to another parable. There was a man,
a landowner, who planted a vineyard; he fenced it
round, dug a winepress in it and built a tower; then he
leased it to tenants and went abroad. When vintage
time drew near he sent his servants to the tenants to
collect his produce. But the tenants seized his servants,
thrashed one, killed another and stoned a third.*

Gn 37:3-4, 12-13, 17-28; Mt 21:33-43, 45-46

✠

Today's two stories about maltreatment of the young are
only superficially - but charmingly - parallel. The first
circles round sibling rivalry. A good case can be made that
Joseph's cheek to his elder brothers was fairly requited,
though it also looks as if the brothers wanted to eliminate
daddy's darling. He amply gets his own back later, teasing
and tormenting his brothers when they come begging
for supplies and fail to recognise this grand Egyptian
functionary. The careful eye will detect that two versions
are here combined. The 'sons of Israel' want to kill Joseph,
but Reuben thinks it enough to give him a cool off in an
empty water hole; the 'sons of Jacob' want to kill him,
but Judah suggests merely selling him. Are the merchants

Midianites or Ishmaelites? Such differences in detail are typical of oral storytelling, and the fact of two versions enhances rather than detracts from the likelihood of the event. This incident would have important consequences: the move to Egypt and 430 years there, followed by the Exodus and the Covenant.

In the Gospel story Jesus' meaning is pegged out by the clear allusions to Isaiah's lovely poem of the disappointed vineyard owner (*Is* 5:1-7). The chief priests and elders could not fail to see themselves cast in the role of the wicked tenants. Matthew clarifies the message even more than the original version in Mark by sending not a whole series of individual messengers, but just two groups of messengers; they obviously correspond to the earlier and later prophets respectively. He also neatly reverses the order: in Mark the son is killed and his body thrown out of the vineyard; in Matthew he is thrown out and killed, as Jesus was crucified outside the city. Matthew also adds to the original parable that the new tenants to whom the owner gives the vineyard will successfully pay their dues to the owner - he often has just such a little touch which shows that he is keeping the Church in mind, and that the Church will bear fruit.

Just how explicit was the prophecy on Jesus' lips? The evangelists may certainly have clarified the prophecy, but how much did Jesus know? As a man he had a human mind, and must have learnt in the same way as any human being. We see his perceptive questions as a boy in the Temple. He was a prophet and so had a prophet's light and insight into reality. Seeing that he must complete his mission by showing the vanity of the Temple cult and all associated with it, he must have known that conflict would follow, that persecution and suffering were his lot. This parable makes it hard to deny that it would lead to death - unless, as some scholars hold, Jesus did not use allegories, and did not intend one-to-one correspondence of the details in his parables. It also gives us precious insight into his treasured relationship with his Father.

Action:

Do I really accept with willing confidence what the Father may send me in the future? Say a prayer for openness to the future and for perseverance.

Saturday

While he was still a long way off, his father saw him and was moved with pity. He ran to the boy, clasped him in his arms and kissed him tenderly. Then his son said, "Father, I have sinned against heaven and against you. I no longer deserve to be called your son."

Mi 7:14-15, 18-20; Lk 15:1-3, 11-32

✠

Most of the Book of Micah, from which the first reading is taken, consists of warnings by the prophet in the eighth century BC, a contemporary of Isaiah of Jerusalem. This passage, however, is more hopeful, promising the return and forgiveness of Israel, and praising God for the forgiveness he had always promised. It makes a fitting background to the parable of the Prodigal Son.

Turning back to the Lord in repentance and God's willing offer of forgiveness constitute an important theme throughout Luke's writings. In the Lukan account of the call of the first disciples (*Lk* 5:1-11) Peter must first admit that he is a sinner before Jesus calls him. In the Passion Story Peter again repents and weeps "bitterly" for his betrayal of his Master. Every speech of the apostles in the Acts of the Apostles ends with a call to repentance. This whole movement is, so to speak, summed up in this parable.

The prodigal son himself is just about as degraded as could be. He insults his father by saying, practically, that he wants his money, whether the father is living or dead, then he squanders the money and works for an unclean gentile, looking after unclean animals. He decides to go home not from any praiseworthy repentance or because he wants to rejoin the family, but simply because he is dead hungry. The father is insanely forgiving, posted to see the youth from afar, running in a most undignified way to greet him, interrupting his pretty little speech of return, giving him a ring (which will enable him to squander yet more money), and slaughtering a calf big enough to feed not merely the family, but the whole village. He behaves in the same way to the stay-at-home son, actually leaving his table guests in order to urge him to come to the festivities. Such is the Father's eagerness to regain this son too. And what of the 'dutiful' son? He begrudges the boy's welcome, refuses to go in, calls him "your son" (not "my brother"), invents stories about prostitutes, and - in his turn - insults his father by lecturing him with brimming anger, refusing to recognise that his dead brother has come to life again.

The characterisation shows Luke at his best, contrasting sharply with Matthew's crisp story of the Two Sons (21:28-31), with its black and white characters, who change their minds and positions for no apparent reason. Luke also gives us that delightful feature of the puzzled anti-hero discussing with himself what he should do next - just like the Rich Fool (*Lk* 12:17-18), the Crafty Steward (16:3-4), the Unjust Judge (18:4). But even this serves its purpose, assuring us that it is not that easy to settle for repentance. It requires not only self-knowledge, but also courage and decision.

Action:

Perhaps it is far enough into Lent to consider our own position, to discuss this with oneself and take part in a Reconciliation Service.

Third Sunday of Lent

It is not easy to die even for a good man - though
of course for someone really worthy, a man might be
prepared to die - but what proves that God loves us
is that Christ died for us while we were still sinners.

Ex 17:3-7; *Rm* 5:1-2, 5-8; *Jn* 4:5-42

✠

On this third Sunday of Lent the cycle of Gospel readings from John begins about the great mysteries of Easter, Jesus' gift of living water, of light and of life. Each of these is a vivid preparation for the climax of the Easter Vigil. They are commented elsewhere!

Moving through salvation history in the first readings, after Adam and Abraham on the first and second Sundays, we come to Moses. Appropriately to the Gospel of living water, the passage chosen is about Moses striking water from the rock - and Paul, with a piece of Jewish allegorisation, tells us that the rock is Christ. Since the story comes twice during the Exodus wanderings, each time in a different geographical place, Paul sees Christ as the rock following them through the desert (*1 Co* 10:4). The desert wanderings form the beginning of the relationship, the stormy love affair between God and his Chosen People, Israel. Throughout the Bible these travels are seen in two different lights, either as the blissful honeymoon period when Israel, spouse of the Lord, bonded with God, or as the first desertions, when Israel defected from God and needed to be brought back in repentance. Hence the place names Massah and Meribah, which signify temptation and strife. On the second occasion, in Numbers 20:11-13, Moses earned his exclusion from the Holy Land, which he was never allowed to enter. He struck the rock twice, and this is understood as expressing disbelief. Some scholars think this punishment disproportionate to such a small offence, and think that Moses did something so utterly terrible that the tradition could not mention it. Whatever the details, we may consider the wanderings through the desert as a mirror of our own relationship with God, heartfelt promises alternating with abject failures.

In his Letter to the Romans Paul reflects first on the human race sunk in sin and rotten in iniquity (chapters 1-3), and then on the saving faith of Abraham in the promise of God (chapter 4). In today's reading he seems to be reflecting on the three great virtues of faith, hope and love. But by themselves they cannot earn salvation. It is only "through our Lord Jesus Christ, by faith that we are judged righteous and at peace with God" - by his death. Paul has many metaphors for this: redemption, reconciliation, ransom. But how does this work? Some have thought that Jesus himself suffered the pains of the damned on our behalf, or that his suffering paid to the devil a debt we should have paid, like a whipping boy who takes the punishment due to a princeling. This is the very paradigm of injustice - that the innocent should suffer for the guilty. And how can God rejoice in pain, especially the pain of his own Son? No, God is not punishing his Son. It is the moment of the most perfect union in loving obedience as Jesus accepts the agony of the cross imposed by his mission of proclaiming the Kingship of God.

Action:

Start a reflective reading of Romans 5-8, not too fast, not too much at a time, a few verses each day.

Monday

Jesus came to Nazara and spoke to the people in the synagogue: "I tell you solemnly, no prophet is ever accepted in his own country."

2 K 5:1-15; Lk 4:24-30

✠

The attractive story of the cure of Naaman the Syrian prepares for the Gospel reading, so that we know what Jesus is talking about. It is the story of a national hero submitting himself in faith (not without persuasion) to the Word of the Lord, given through Elisha. It is a pity that we cannot include among the readings also the story of Elijah and the widow of Zarephath (*1 K* 17:7-16): in the great drought Elijah asked her for the last crumbs/drops of food supplies that she had. Generously she responded and as a reward "jar of meal was not spent nor the jug of oil emptied" until the rain came.

However, the weight of the readings falls upon the story in Luke of Jesus' opening proclamation in the synagogue at Nazareth. The solemn opening of the scene is read on a Sunday in Year C: Jesus, filled with the Spirit, announces his programme, the programme exemplified in the Gospel of Luke, to bring salvation to the whole world. Salvation is not the prerogative of the Jews, but Jesus and his disciples will bring it to the gentiles. It is difficult for us, in a one-world situation, to envisage how revolutionary an idea this was for the Jews, for to them the worship of the Lord was their own national treasure, shared with no one else. Luke, however, is writing for a gentile audience in the greater world of the Eastern Roman Empire, and he stresses everywhere that Jesus is "a light for revelation to the gentiles" as well as "for the glory of your people Israel", as Simeon puts it (2:28). So gentiles from outside are invited to share the great supper with Israel, and the Samaritans, the most hated neighbours, are put forward as the model: it is a Samaritan leper who returns to thank Jesus for the cure, while the nine Jews just walk away. It is a Samaritan traveller who helps the wounded man, beaten up on the road, while the Jewish priest and Levite pass by on the other side. Then in the Acts of the Apostles Luke goes on to show the spread of the Good News to Samaria, then the incorporation of the gentile centurion Cornelius at Caesarea, then the spread of the Gospel to "the ends of the earth", namely Rome. He stresses also how the Jews themselves refused to accept Paul's message, and indeed blocked it, first in Asia Minor, then in Greece and finally in Rome.

In his opening proclamation Jesus shows that there is precedent for both of these, both the refusal by the Jews and acceptance by the gentiles, in the stories of Elijah and Elisha. For Christians of today a comparable question arises. Are we wholehearted in our service of God, or is real holiness, real self-sacrifice, real attention to the needy to be found outside Christianity as much as or more than within the Christian Church and ourselves?

Action:

Bring the healing of Christ to somebody wounded or sick.

Tuesday

Peter went up to Jesus and said, "Lord, how often must I forgive my brother if he wrongs me? As often as seven times?" Jesus answered, "Not seven, I tell you, but seventy-seven times."

Dn 3:25, 34-43; Mt 18:21-35

✠

The first reading is the prayer of Azariah, the companion of Daniel. It is the first prayer of the Three Young Men cast into the furnace of blazing fire because they refused to obey the order of King Nebuchadnezzar to worship him. The second prayer, often called the Canticle of Creation, is more familiar; it calls on all creation to praise the Lord. This first prayer is deeply imbued with the post-exilic spirituality of guilt and, repentance and longing for forgiveness. It prepares us for the parable of the Unforgiving Debtor.

We may see the importance of forgiveness from the Lord's Prayer: forgiveness is the only obligation which Matthew stresses by repetition at the end of the prayer. We should never risk saying that prayer without an examination of conscience. The importance of this parable cannot be fully appreciated without knowledge of its context. In his

Gospel Matthew, a well-organised and gifted teacher, gathers together items of the teaching of Jesus into five discourses, each treating different aspects of the Christian life. He probably used a collection of Sayings of the Lord, which is mentioned by early Christian writers, but which later disappeared completely (perhaps because most of it was already available in Matthew and Luke, so that there was no point in copying it out separately). This fourth discourse is concerned with behaviour to one another within the community, and it is striking that almost half of it concentrates on forgiveness, suggesting that this is the most important single aspect of living in community - and perhaps of marriage and family as well. There are always bound to be offences and misunderstandings. Swift apology and forgiveness can not only wipe out the offence, but even leave the relationship stronger than it was in the first place. This may be reinforced by the observation that it is always the stronger person who is the first to apologise and the first to forgive.

The parable is told in typical Matthaean fashion. At the basis there is a contrast between two different characters; just as in the parable of the Two Sons (21:28-32), or the Ten Wedding Attendants (25:1-12) or the final parable of the Sheep and Goats (25:31-46), here the two Debtors are contrasted. Then there are the over-the-top contrasting sums of money: ten thousand talents is an astronomical sum, many times the tribute of any Roman province at this time. No modern scale is possible, for our expenditures are now so different: at that time there were no foreign holidays, washing machines or superyachts to buy! There is no question of any individual ever paying it back, no matter how long he languished in prison. On the other hand a hundred denarii is the wages for a few days of casual labour.

Action:

Are you sure that you are not holding a grudge against anyone? If so, untie the knot!

Wednesday

The Law or the Prophets. I have come not to abolish
but to complete them. I tell you solemnly, till heaven
and earth disappear, not one dot, not one little stroke,
shall disappear from the Law until its purpose
is achieved.

Dt 4:1, 5-9; Mt 5:17-19

✠

Both of today's readings insist on the importance of the exact observance of the Law. What can this mean, and why does the Church put it before us with such force? Immediately after the Gospel passage comes some explanation, for Jesus says that our way of observing the Law must go deeper than that of the scribes and Pharisees. (The Pharisees were renowned for observing not merely the written laws, but also the traditional interpretation of them, supposedly handed down by word of mouth from the time of Moses. The scribes - the Greek word literally means 'writers', so they must have been among the small proportion of the population who were literate - were the lawyers, skilled at reaching a solution when two laws clashed.) But after this Matthew gives us six examples of ways in which Jesus' moral teaching does deepen the Law.

This is, however, an opportunity to reflect on the way in which Christian teaching depends on and grows from that of Judaism. So many of the major concepts of the New Testament are built on those of the Old Testament; we might mention creation, the spirit and the covenant. Fundamental to the Old Testament is the idea of creation by God: everything depends upon God, and man and woman are created in the image of God to continue God's act of creation and to conserve and develop what God has made. In the New Testament this idea is taken up into the idea of a new creation in Christ, by which creation reaches its fullness and is to be utterly filled with the divinity. As Christ the Word is the principle of creation, in whom all creation occurred, so the Risen Christ is the principle and fullness of all things in the new creation.

At the creation the spirit of God hovered over the waters. From time to time the spirit of God seized upon the leaders of the people, leading them to victory, or on the prophets of the people, leading them to a clearer vision of God's purposes. In the New Testament this Spirit is seen to be a divine Person, proceeding from the Father through the Son, a Helper, the Spirit of the Son, making Christ present when he is physically absent.

The Covenant made by God with Moses and his rabble of runaway slaves on Sinai was the marriage bond by which God bound himself to his spouse, Israel. Israel broke this covenant by infidelity, described in terms of prostitution and marital infidelity, and God drew them back to himself. When Israel's idolatry finally shattered the marriage bond and led them into exile, they began to look forward to a new covenant in spirit and in truth. This is the new relationship established by Jesus at the Last Supper, of which the Eucharist is a perpetual memorial.

Action:

How important is that prayer, "Come, Holy Spirit, fill the hearts of your faithful, and kindle in them the fire of your love." As we struggle to deepen our understanding during Lent, it bears frequent repetition.

Thursday

Jesus was casting out a devil and it was dumb; but
when the devil had gone out the dumb man spoke,
and the people were amazed. But some of them said,
"It is through Beelzebul, the prince of devils, that he
casts out devils."

Jr 7:23-28; *Lk* 11:14-23

✠

The context of the reading from Jeremiah helps us to appreciate its force. It comes in the Book of Jeremiah as one of a series of complaints about worship in the Temple. Jeremiah complains that the Temple worship is insincere and mixed up with idolatry. Anyway, says the prophet just before this reading, I, the Lord, never asked for sacrifice from you; what I want is sincerity and obedience. We simply do not know how much idol worship there was at this time in Israel. We know that there was a good deal, for Jeremiah mentions elaborate offerings made to Astarte, the Queen of Heaven, which are absolutely incompatible with the worship of the Lord. There was always in Israel a leaning towards worship of fertility gods on the tops of the mountains. Without the modern knowledge of the processes of reproduction, and with the high rate of infant mortality, it was obviously tempting to be drawn towards magical and superstitious practices to increase fertility. Even in modern times there seems to be room for a good deal of superstition in apparently Christian cultures (black cats, the number thirteen).

In the Gospel passage Jesus also is accused of being in league with the Prince of Demons. The name of the Prince of Demons, 'Beelzebul', has never been satisfactorily explained; it might possibly mean 'Lord of the Earth'. Some versions have it as 'Beelezbub', meaning 'Lord of the flies', which could be a deliberately abusive alteration, rather like calling the Golden Bull worshipped in the desert a 'golden calf'.

However, the interest of the passage is that, by ascribing Jesus' exorcisms to the Prince of Demons, his opponents are at least admitting that he did cast out demons. In the primitive state of medical knowledge at the time diseases could often be ascribed to demonic possession. Some diseases are of course psychosomatic. In the Bible the description of what is noted as 'leprosy' would include such illnesses as psoriasis, which is psychosomatic. It is impossible to calculate the effect on a person suffering from a psychosomatic illness of a confrontation with the powerful and awesome personality of Jesus. Such an encounter might have an immediate and stunningly effective outcome. We have no records other than the

Gospels of the effects of encounter with a man who is also God! What is the effect of meeting a divine person? The Gospels are trying to give an account of such meetings. On the purely evidential level, it would be ridiculous to reduce all Jesus' miracles to the level of psychological cures. They are framed to show that Jesus is not a merely human person.

Action:

Spend some time in prayer, perhaps before the Blessed Sacrament, in wonder at the healing power of the Risen Christ among us.

Friday

*Jesus replied, "This is the first: Listen, Israel, the Lord
our God is the one Lord, and you must love the Lord
your God with all your heart, with all your soul,
with all your mind and with all your strength."*

Ho 14:2-10; Mk 12:28-34

✠

The first reading gives us a wonderfully encouraging
passage from Hosea, promising a sort of super-fertile,
super-green Garden of Eden if Israel will return to the
Lord in love and loyalty. The Garden of Eden in the story
of Genesis may of course be regarded as a representation
of what humanity *should be* and *will be* in the end, rather
than what humanity *was* in the beginning. Hosea is the
prophet of God's love, shot through with the imagery
of God's espousal to Israel and affection for Israel, but
nevertheless marked by reproaches at Israel's frequent
betrayals. This positive final passage of Hosea joins well
with the Gospel reading.

The Gospel reading presents us with the most positive
of all Jesus' encounters with the Jewish leaders. It has
already been suggested that Jesus may well have been
close to the Pharisees (p.45). This passage shows an

amicable discussion with a Pharisee lawyer. In Mark's account, the original version, there is no suggestion that the lawyer was trying to trick Jesus; he was just asking this teacher a typical Jewish question about priorities.

Jesus replies with an impeccable rabbinic answer, bringing together two texts from different books of the Bible. The first, about love of God, is from the basic confession of faith in Deuteronomy 6:5, recited by every faithful Jew three times a day, "You shall love the Lord your God with all your heart, mind and strength", as straightforward a priority as you could wish. But the exciting thing about the answer is that Jesus couples that with another text from Leviticus 19:18, "You shall love your neighbour as yourself". The command is not new, but it is only staggering that Jesus puts it on a level with the other; it will, of course, in all his discussions be his main principle in interpreting the Law.

Perhaps more striking still is that Jesus uses a strictly rabbinic argument to couple the two. The rules of interpretation were codified by the great Rabbi Hillel a few years after Jesus' birth, and one of them is that a formula in one text should be used to interpret the same formula in another. These are the only two texts in the Bible where the formula "and you shall love" occurs, and Jesus uses that coincidence as the basis of his exegesis. It is no wonder that the lawyer/scribe congratulates him on this fine, orthodox piece of interpretation. Jesus was no raw peasant, relying on earthy country wisdom; he was up with the best of them in learned technique of interpretation of the Law. His gracious reply to the lawyer rounds off the discussion with fitting dignity.

Action:

It is so easy to instruct someone in such a way that the learner feels a fool. Try teaching someone a way of life which will ease life - in such a way that the learner feels great!

Saturday

Two men went up to the Temple to pray, one a Pharisee, the other a tax collector. The Pharisee stood there and said this prayer to himself, "I thank you, God, that I am not grasping, unjust, adulterous like the rest of mankind, and particularly that I am not like this tax collector here." The tax collector stood some distance away, not daring even to raise his eyes to heaven; but he beat his breast and said, "God, be merciful to me, a sinner."

Ho 5:15-6:6; *Lk* 18:9-14

✠

The Solemnity of the Annunciation to Mary falls on this day. It has its own readings, but we continue our reflections on the Lenten readings set for the day.

In the earliest tradition the Resurrection is described as being "on the third day, in accordance with the scriptures". Does this simply mean that the Resurrection was in accordance with the whole thrust of the scriptures that God would protect his Messiah (an interpretation, for example, of *Ps* 21), or again of Jesus' three great prophecies of the Passion and Resurrection (*Mk* 8:31; 9:31; 10:32-34)? The element of timing may refer more specifically to today's passage in Hosea, "after a day or two he will bring us back to life, on the third day he will raise us" as fulfilment of Scripture. Certainly the final sentence, "what I want is love not sacrifice" was constantly in Jesus' mind, and determined all his understanding of the Law. In Matthew it is referred to three times (9:13; 12:7; 23:23). The love which Jesus here requires is no vague feeling of good will or attraction. It is the self-sacrificing love of parent for child who will stick by the child whatever the cost. In a family I may not get on very well with my brother, but in the last analysis I will always come to his rescue in the love of a devoted family.

Luke is the evangelist of prayer, offering frequent hints about it. In his Gospel Jesus is explicitly mentioned as being in prayer more often than in any other, at the Baptism, the Transfiguration, when called upon to teach his disciples the Lord's Prayer (3:21; 6:12; 11:1). The Agony in the Garden is shaped to show the need for prayer in time of testing (22:40). In the Infancy Narratives his characters burst into prayerful praise on every occasion, and from these we derive the three great canticles of the Church, the *Magnificat*, the *Benedictus* and the *Nunc dimittis*. His parables insist on the need for perseverance in prayer, especially the parables of the Friend at Midnight (11:9-12) and the Unjust Judge (18:1-5). Their motives may not be perfect: the Friend at Midnight eventually caves in because he does not want to be shamed for inhospitable behaviour when the whole village hears the hammering on the door. And the appellant to the Unjust Judge seems to be on the edge of violence, threatening to hit the Judge in the face! Today, in this parable of the Pharisee and the Tax Collector, Luke combines humour with deadly earnestness. The pompous and self-contradictory bragging of innocence by the Pharisee is duly repellent, while the humble self-accusation of the tax collector is something to which we can all aspire.

Action:

Is this an occasion to examine whether I have kept up my Lenten resolutions of prayer?

Fourth Sunday of Lent

*You were darkness once, but now you are light
in the Lord; be like children of light.*

1 S 16:1, 6-7, 10-13; *Ep* 5:8-14; *Jn* 9:1-41

☩

Today's Gospel reading narrates Jesus' cure of the blind man in the Temple, and the stubborn blindness of the Temple authorities, in preparation for the new light at Easter, symbolised by the paschal candle.

In our advance on the Sundays of Lent through the story of Israel we have reached the formation of the kingship in Israel. David is revered as the founder of the dynasty which will issue in the Messiah, the Anointed King of the House of David. He is revered also as the founder of the liturgy, for he bought the land on which the Temple was to be built, though he was not allowed to build it himself, being a 'man of blood'. He was revered also as the author of the Psalms, since, in one of the other stories of his rise to power, he was the musician who soothed his predecessor Saul in Saul's moods of black despair. There is also the story of David and Goliath. These three stories of his rise are difficultly inter-compatible, and clash also with the stories of his separate anointings as King of Judah and King of Israel. Stories of the youth of a hero are often historically shaky. What a king! Brave, charismatic, charming, but also unscrupulous, cunning and grossly indulgent to his own family. Should he be dismissed as an oversexed bandit, or is his repentance greater than his sin of adultery with Bathsheba and his murder of her husband?

The point of this story is that God chooses whom he will. Primogeniture was powerful in Israel, but God is not bound by it in his choice. The younger Abel was more pleasing than the older Cain. Jacob wrested the blessing of succession from his elder brother Esau by not fussing too much about the truth. Joseph rescued his brothers from famine. God chooses his own messengers, and they are not always the most obvious people.

The Letter to the Ephesians, which provides the second reading, is one of the later letters of the Pauline corpus. No longer dealing with the problems of the Law in Christianity or the fractious community at Corinth, it takes a wider view of the lordship of Christ. Here it quotes an early Christian hymn of Christ as the rising sun, which prepares us for the Gospel reading about Christ as the light. The sun has always been a traditional image of God, as it gives warmth and life on earth, and enables us to see, understand and relax! Already in Zechariah's canticle, the *Benedictus* Jesus is heralded as "the rising sun to give light to those who live in darkness and the shadow of death". So traditionally also churches are built to face the rising sun in the East, and, especially in the Eastern Greek Church the Sacrament of Baptism and Confirmation is known as *photismos* or 'enlightenment', as the light of Christ comes to shine on the new Christian.

Action:

In Judaism there is a saying "A Sabbath without a guest is no Sabbath". Why not invite a lonely person to Sunday lunch?

Monday

*Now there was a court official there whose son was ill
at Capernaum and, hearing that Jesus had arrived in
Galilee from Judaea, he went and asked him to come
and cure his son as he was at the point of death. Jesus
said, "So you will not believe unless you see signs
and portents!"*

Is 65:17-21; Jn 4:43-54

✠

The part of Isaiah from which the first reading is taken
comes from the latest period of the Book of Isaiah, after
the return from Exile. It is full of joy and gladness at the
return and in the vivid hope of the coming of the Messiah.
Awareness is becoming more and more clear that this will
mean redemption and renewal not only to Israel, but to all
nations who will come to draw salvation from Jerusalem.
The particular link to the Gospel reading seems to be "No
child shall there be who lives but a few days", referring to
the son of the official at Capernaum who is to be raised
from his dire sickness.

The story of the official's son comes in three of the
Gospels (not Mark), with slight variations. Here, in John's
account, it is the son of a court official, which fits the

fact that Galilee in the time of Jesus was ruled by Herod Antipas, who boasted an extensive court - it was for their entertainment that he had John the Baptist beheaded. In the Matthew/Luke tradition it is a centurion, possibly Roman, but more likely a gentile mercenary. Luke stresses that he had earned the attention of Jesus by paying for the building of a synagogue (still visible under the later, reconstructed synagogue at Capernaum on the shore of the Lake of Galilee). In each tradition the official is the paradigm of gentile faith in Jesus.

For the remainder of Lent all the Gospel readings, with one exception, are taken from John. The Passion reading on Good Friday is also that of John. Clearly it is an indication that the Gospel of John has a special relevance for the mysteries of Easter.

At the end of the account of the cure of the boy John mentions that this was the second sign given by Jesus. The first twelve chapters of John contain seven signs, and are often known as 'the Book of Signs', for in John the miracles of Jesus have a subtly different sense from that of the other Gospels. In the other Gospels the miracles show the beginning of the Kingship of God, Jesus triumphing over disease, blindness, alienation and death, and so ushering in the Kingship of God. In John the miracles are often explicitly called 'signs' and they are signs of spiritual values and of Jesus' own glory. Thus the first sign at Cana, the conversion of the water of Jewish purification into wine, is a sign of the wedding feast of the Messiah, the joyful union of God with his people. Our present story is the second sign, the gift of life. In John life always has at least the overtones of eternal life, for Jesus has come to give eternal life. In the same way the gift of life to the Blind Man in the Temple is a sign both of the glory of Jesus and of the enlightenment he gives, the understanding of Jesus as the Son of God: "as the Father raises the dead and gives them life, so the Son gives life to anyone he chooses…so that all may honour the Son as they honour the Father" (*Jn* 5:21-22).

Action:

Can you count up seven signs of God's love for you in your life?

Tuesday

One man there had an illness which had lasted thirty-eight years, and when Jesus saw him lying there and knew he had been in this condition for a long time, he said, "Do you want to be well again?" "Sir," replied the sick man "I have no one to put me into the pool when the water is disturbed; and while I am still on the way, someone else gets there before me."

Ezk 47:1-9, 12; Jn 5:1-3, 5-16

✠

The Holy Land is hot and dry; water is a perpetual problem. If you stand on the large raised area, built up for the Jerusalem Temple by King Herod the Great, and look to the east on your right, you may see the Desert of Judaea. More likely you will see little, but a heat haze. There is a little stream, the Wadi Kedron, flowing in that direction towards the Dead Sea; normally it peters out in the heat of the desert before it reaches the Sea. The Dead Sea is an uncongenial stretch of salt water, with plenty of other noxious and smelly chemicals too - no birds, no living things, no life; it is well named! Against this background Ezekiel's vision is thrilling: a fresh stream emerging from the Temple, growing in volume and fertility as it flows.

Fruit trees with new fruit every month. The stream will even make it possible for fish to live in the Sea. Wonder of wonders, there will be fishermen all round the sea! It is impossible to imagine anything more enticing. This is the image of the new life which the restoration of Israel will impart, the life of the messianic times. Such is the promise which Ezekiel gave to the exiles in Babylon, far from their homes and homeland, deprived of everything they had ever valued.

Shift the scene back to Jerusalem, but keep the same problem: water. On the gentle slope running down from the north into the Temple there is an artificial reservoir to gather the water flowing off the hillsides for a short time after heavy rains. Surrounding it are five colonnades - or rather four colonnades surrounding and one across the middle, dividing it into two pools. This is called the Pool of Bethzatha, and part of the steps down into it still exists - the author of the Gospel knows his Jerusalem well. Around the Pool are still the remains of little healing shrines, for it was obviously a place where sick and disabled people came expecting to be healed.

Jesus comes to the Pool and takes pity on one sufferer who has been waiting thirty eight years - and all the authorities can do is complain that he should not 'work' on the Sabbath! The first three Gospels give Jesus only one visit to Jerusalem, just at the end of his ministry, but in John there are four visits, the first for the Cleansing of the Temple at the very beginning of his ministry. Then on the next visits the authorities are thirsting to catch him out and arrest him, but find no opportunity till the end. With the wider view of the Jerusalem ministry provided by John we can see Jesus acting in Jerusalem as he did in Galilee. Again, his interpretation of the Law is the same: no Sabbath obligation can stand in the way of Jesus' love and care for individuals.

These two stories of water and healing prepare us for the healing, life-giving waters of Baptism, celebrated at the Easter Vigil on Holy Saturday.

Action:

What sort of healing do I need? What is my particular disability which blocks the flow of living water?

Wednesday

For the Father loves the Son
and shows him everything he does himself,
and he will show him even greater things than these,
works that will astonish you.

Is 49:8-15; Jn 5:17-30

✠

The first reading from Isaiah is a cheerful hymn, promising the return of the exiles from Babylon to Jerusalem. The return is depicted here and elsewhere in terms of the journey of forty years across the desert - except that it will be a triumphal journey through rich pastures, "a highway of all the mountains, and the high roads banked up". Not only that, but the pilgrims will gather from every direction. All this is fulfilling God's promises which can never fail, for "Does a woman forget her baby at the breast or fail to cherish the son of her womb? Yet even if these forget, I will never forget you."

The Gospel reading from John follows on directly from yesterday's reading. We left Jesus being attacked by "the Jews" for working on the Sabbath. They were especially nettled at Jesus claiming the right to work on the Sabbath because only God has to work on the Sabbath - babies are born (he has to give them life) and people die (he has to judge them).

The passage which follows is perhaps the clearest and most elevated statement of the relationship between Father and Son in the Gospels. The classic definitions of the early Councils are couched in terms of Greek philosophy, static definitions. This definition is a dynamic definition, that is, in terms of function and will and power. This is much more in line with Hebrew ways of thinking and explaining. At beginning and end the passage is bracketed by the statement that Father and Son have the same will: there is no distinction in what they desire and do: whatever the Father does, the Son does too (v. 19), and "I seek not to do my own will but the will of him who sent me" (v. 30). In more detail, to give life is the supreme prerogative of God, for no one else can give life. But just as the Father gives life, so the Son gives life (v. 21 and 25). Only the power to give life comes to the Son from the Father (v. 26). This does not mean that the Son is inferior to the Father; far from it, for they both have the same power, though in the Son it is a derivative power.

Similarly, it is also the prerogative of God to judge (v. 22 and 27). The Father judges no one, but has given all judgement to the Son. But the Son, in his turn, judges no one, for throughout the Gospel we see human beings judging themselves by their reaction to Jesus. But here again, the Son's power to judge, though total and absolute, is derivative, for the Father "has entrusted all judgement to the Son so that all may honour the Son as they honour the Father."

A little analogy might help: a son has been taught to drive a car by his father and uses all the same techniques (right or wrong!). Desperate to justify himself with mother beside him, he parks the car exactly as dad would park. "You are your father's son", she remarks.

Action:

Do I judge others and those around me with the same compassion and tolerance as that which I expect to receive from my Father in heaven?

Thursday

Were I to testify on my own behalf,
my testimony would not be valid;
but there is another witness who can speak on my behalf,
and I know that his testimony is valid.

Ex 32:7-14; Jn 5:31-47

✠

The Gospel reading points out how the opponents of Jesus put their trust in Moses, and the first reading illustrates this. Hardly had the Covenant between God and the Hebrews been completed when they turned away to an idol. The idol they made is described as a golden calf, but it was really a golden bull. The god Baal is often depicted as standing on a bull, hurling a thunderbolt, for he was a weather god. Baal was widely worshipped; Psalm 28 (29) was originally a psalm to Baal, the thunder god ("The voice of the Lord, shattering the cedars" - originally "the voice of Baal…"); the psalm, originally used to worship Baal, was adapted for the worship of the Lord. In the narrative of Exodus the idol is described as a calf to belittle it. In any case, it was the prayer of Moses which averted the deserved punishment from the Lord, so "you put your hope in Moses", for liberation from deserved punishment in their own era also.

The Gospel reading continues the readings of Tuesday and Wednesday on the confrontation of Jesus with the Jewish leaders in the Temple. Jesus cites his testimonies which bear witness to him. First the testimony of John. This was especially important because John had been so revered by the people that when, in the synoptic Gospels, Jesus is challenged about his own authority he replies, asking them to explain John's authority, and they do not dare to answer, for John had been so revered. The Gospels represent the beheading of the Baptist as a palace-party-gone-wrong. The Jewish historian Josephus, however, says that Herod Antipas imprisoned John because he was afraid that he would start a rebellion; he obviously had a considerable following.

The second testimony is that of the works which the Father has given Jesus. In the synoptic Gospels the wonderful works of Jesus in healing, restoring, gathering in sinners and outcasts, are all manifestations of the coming of the Kingship of God. In the Gospel of John they are signs that Jesus is doing the work of the Father. The third witness is the testimony of the Father. Since they do not receive this testimony, "his word finds no home in you" (v. 38), this is perhaps the internal witness of God in the conscience.

The fourth witness is the scriptures. In the formation of the New Testament the fulfilment of the scriptures was particularly important. Even the oldest creedal testimony, given by Paul in 1 Corinthians 15:3-5, twice mentions "according to the scriptures" - both Jesus' death and his Resurrection. The constant recurrence of Old Testament witness shows that the disciples must have made a collection of texts which were fulfilled by the life of Jesus. This passage is an important witness to the claims of Jesus.

Action:

Is my life really a witness to Jesus? Do others find in me the image of God and a member of the Body of Christ?

Friday

Then, as Jesus taught in the Temple, he cried out:
"Yes, you know me and you know where I came from.
Yet I have not come of myself:
no, there is one who sent me and I really come from him,
and you do not know him".

Ws 2:1, 12-22; Jn 7:1-2, 10, 25-30

✠

The Book of Wisdom is one of the latest books of the Old
Testament, written by the Jews of Alexandria, possibly as
late as the first century BC. In the title it is ascribed to King
Solomon. The tradition of Wisdom goes back to Solomon,
so he may be regarded in some way as being behind the
Book, but the actual writing was certainly several centuries
later. The first part of the Book consists of confrontations
between Lady Wisdom and Lady Folly (a prostitute), each
questing for followers and setting out their own recipe
for happiness. Here we have a passage of Folly sneering
at the efforts of the conscientious virtuous person. It is
remarkable that the very same words are made their own
by the Jewish leaders when they mock and sarcastically
challenge Jesus on the cross (*Mt* 27:40-43).

In the Gospel reading we have moved to another confrontation between Jesus and the leaders of the Jews: he has gone up to Jerusalem for the annual Festival of Tabernacles. On this festival the custom was (and is) to spend the time not in the houses, but in a leafy booth (probably attached to the house) in commemoration of the time spent in tents and temporary shelters during the desert wanderings. "The Jews" still cannot take control of him "because his Hour has not yet come". This "Hour" provides a thread running through the Gospel of John. It appears first, and mysteriously, at the marriage feast of Cana, where Jesus initially refuses his mother's request on the grounds that his Hour has not yet come. But what is this Hour? In this controversy on the Festival of Tabernacles it still has not yet come. Later, in prayer, Jesus will wonder whether he should ask to be delivered from his Passion, and rejects the idea because it was for this Hour that he came into the world (*Jn* 12:27-28). Finally, at the beginning of the Last Supper, he sees that the Hour has come (13:1). It is the Hour of his Glorification (17:1-2) when he is to be lifted up from the earth. With typical Johannine ambiguity this 'lifting up' is both physical, exalted onto the cross, and metaphorical, exalted and glorified by and with his Father.

A word must be said about the expression 'the Jews' in the narrative. Some have said that - to avoid the appearance of blanket anti-Semitism - it should be translated 'the authorities of the Jews'. However in fact it is used differently in different parts of the narrative. Scholars have established that the Gospel of John underwent several different editions. In the earliest, factual edition, the expression is used simply geographically, of 'inhabitants of Judaea'. In later editions it is used as a sort of keyword for the opposition to Jesus, those Jews who did not accept him.

Action:

Is sarcasm one of my weapons? Is it an effective way of learning? Is it a Christian way of approaching a problem?

Saturday

> *"Does not scripture say that the Christ must be*
> *descended from David and come from the town*
> *of Bethlehem?" So the people could not agree about*
> *him. Some would have liked to arrest him, but no one*
> *actually laid hands on him.*

Jr 11:18-20; *Jn* 7:40-52

✠

Jeremiah is here bemoaning the treatment he received from his fellow countrymen for warning them during the siege of Jerusalem by the Babylonians that the city would be destroyed unless they turned back to the Lord. This was considered by the officials to be destructive of morale, and he was arrested and would have been killed if the king had not intervened. The king put him in solitary confinement in an empty storage well, fed on starvation rations - "and into the mud sank Jeremiah" (*Jr* 38:6). It is not always comfortable to speak the truth, neither for Jeremiah nor for Jesus.

In the Gospel reading - a continuation of yesterday's passage - the stubbornness of the opponents of Jesus becomes unmistakable. At first there is still a possibility of mistake, through the mistaken idea that Jesus came from, i.e. originated in, Galilee rather than Bethlehem. This provoked the sardonic comment about lack of prophets in Galilee. The Galilaeans were despised in the rabbinic schools of Jerusalem, to the extent that they were said not even to be able to produce a properly-constructed vow. This may have been a fair comment or a gibe born of rivalry between the rabbinic schools in Jerusalem and Tiberias.

Then the hostility mounts, as the leaders reply with sarcasm to the enthusiastic reverence expressed by the agents they had sent to arrest Jesus. This is followed by a further barrage of sarcasm against one of their own number, Nicodemus, who makes the unimpeachable protest that Jesus should at least be given fair judgement. We have reached the situation where no argument will shake their hostility.

The question whether Jesus was Christ is not stupid. For us "Christ" is almost part of Jesus' name, but at first it was descriptive, and he was "Jesus, the Christ", that is, "Jesus, the Messiah" or "Jesus, the Anointed One". Jesus himself did not accept the title until the final scene before the High Priest. Indeed in Mark 12:35-37 he even raised a difficulty, asking how David (as author of the Psalms) could address his own descendant as "my Lord" in Psalm 110 (109). The title had political overtones, for at the time the Messiah was expected to be a glorious warrior who would sweep the

Roman occupiers into the sea. Jews contemporary to Jesus did not associate the prophecies of the Suffering Servant of the Lord with the Messiah, which was such a strong emphasis in the concept for Jesus himself. This is why at Caesarea Philippi (*Mk* 8:29) he rebukes Peter's declaration and immediately goes on to speak of his coming Passion. It required repeated emphasis before the disciples came to realise that the Son of Man came not to be served, but to serve, and that the followers of Jesus must take up their cross and follow him.

Action:

Do I serve, that is, contribute to the happiness of those who serve me. Gratitude expressed for this service is at least a beginning!

Fifth Sunday of Lent

...if Christ is in you then your spirit is life itself because you have been justified; and if the Spirit of him who raised Jesus from the dead is living in you, then he who raised Jesus from the dead will give life to your own mortal bodies through his Spirit living in you.

Ezk 37:12-14; Rm 8:8-11; Jn 11:1-45

In our progress through the history of salvation on the Sundays of Lent we now come to the final stage, the New Covenant promised by Jeremiah and Ezekiel. As this is the Sunday of the Raising of Lazarus it is appropriate that the Old Testament passage chosen should be the promise of being raised to life. This whole passage of Ezekiel 37:1-14 is a splendid vision of Israel raised to new life (of which we here read only the conclusion). This is in fact a prophecy of the nation being raised to new life in the return from the Exile, rather than a prophecy of personal resurrection, but this Vision of the Valley of the Dead Bones is still a vivid and gripping presage of the personal resurrection of the dead.

In the earlier period of Israel's history there was no concept of resurrection from the dead; the belief develops in the course of the Old Testament. At first it was thought that the dead simply returned to the stock of the ancestors. Then came the idea of Sheol, a place where the dead gathered for a sort of half-life without power, almost like dead leaves, where no one could even praise God. But a yearning to be for ever with God then begins to be felt, and an appreciation that God will somehow deliver his own. This yearning for life with God is particularly strong in Job and in the Psalms. There is no clear idea of rising to new personal life until the early second century BC, and then there are two conceptions: either that only the good will rise again to life (*2 M* 7:9), or that all will rise again, some to everlasting life, some to everlasting shame and disgrace (*Dn* 12:2).

Chapter 8 of Romans is the chapter of the Spirit, where Paul writes more about the Spirit of God living in us than anywhere else; it is also the climax of his explanation of our salvation by being re-born into Christ. This begins in Romans 6, where he teaches that that by faith and Baptism we are plunged ('baptise' means 'dip' or 'plunge' into water) into Christ's death and rise with him to new life. But, as today's reading explains, we have not come back to life, but have gone forward to a new life in the Spirit of God. In the Resurrection our animating spirit will no longer be the human spirit, but the Spirit of God. The Spirit who raised Jesus from the dead is already living in us, and we live with a new Law, the Law of the Spirit, by whom our whole life is transformed.

Action:

Read Romans 8 and see the part which the Spirit should be playing in our Christian life.

Monday

> As they persisted with their question, he looked up and
> said, "If there is one of you who has not sinned, let him
> be the first to throw a stone at her." Then he bent down
> and wrote on the ground again. When they heard this
> they went away one by one, beginning with the
> eldest, until Jesus was left alone with the woman,
> who remained standing there.

Dn 13:1-9, 15-17, 19-30, 33-62; *Jn* 8:1-11

✠

Two stories of sexual misbehaviour are presented to us
today: the story of Susanna, tacked on to the Book of Daniel,
and the story of the Adulterous Woman in the Gospel of
John. First of all it must be remarked that the Bible accepts
the starting point, common at that time and in that area, that
the woman is primarily responsible. This would no longer
be acceptable, at least in Western society - neither is it
accepted in either of these stories. The whole point of the
Susanna story is that Daniel's ploy makes clear that the two
elders were to blame. Similarly in the Gospel story, there
is no evidence that the woman had been to blame; Jesus
apportions no blame and it is the men who shiftily wander
off, and so tacitly admit to not having a clean record.

The story of Susanna, attached to the Book of Daniel, is a classic example of a neat little detective story. There are many legends about a wise man called Daniel, and this story takes up the name, changing it slightly to make it the Hebrew name 'Daniel', which means 'God is my Judge'. By making Daniel so young, the story also integrates the theme that all wisdom comes from God, and that God gives wisdom to whom he will, often the younger. The same theme of God's preference for the younger occurs also in the stories of Cain and Abel, Esau and Jacob and the blessing of David as king, emphasising the sovereignty of God. Daniel's rather pert reply to the two elders whom he has convicted of false testimony makes more sense in Hebrew, for in both cases Daniel's condemnation is a pun on the name of the tree under which they claim to have seen the offence occur; this cannot really be reproduced in translation.

The incident of the Woman taken in Adultery is a little strange in the Gospel of John; it suits much better the synoptic Gospels, perhaps especially Luke, who is the evangelist of repentance and mercy. Jesus treats the woman who weeps on his feet and dries her feet with her tears (*Lk* 7:36-50) with the same delicacy and consideration, leaving her to express her repentance in her own way. His approach to repentant sinners is always warmly welcoming. The style and vocabulary are also much more Lukan than

Johannine. In fact this incident appears in different places in the ancient manuscripts, sometimes at the end of John's Gospel, before settling into its present position. It may have been an isolated ancient story about Jesus, circulating independently.

It would be a mistake to deduce from the story that Jesus could write - still more to guess what he was writing! The Greek word can mean 'write' or 'draw'. Was he just doodling to give the others time to think out their reaction and bring them to the sense of their own sinfulness?

Action:

Is my approach to those who come asking to be forgiven as welcoming and forgiving as that of Jesus? Why not?

Tuesday

So Jesus said:
"When you have lifted up the Son of Man,
then you will know that I am He
and that I do nothing of myself:
what the Father has taught me
is what I preach."

Nb 21:4-9; Jn 8:21-30

✠

The reading from Numbers is introduced as a prelude to
Jesus' saying, "when you have lifted up the Son of Man" in
the Gospel reading. It is a reference to the strange incident
of the bronze serpent lifted up in the desert of Sinai as a
totem for a cure, during the wanderings on Sinai. Is the
Bible supporting superstitious worship? We need not be
surprised that there was superstitious worship in Israel -
that has been mentioned many times - but here it actually
appears in the Bible without negative overtones, as a model
for Jesus being "lifted up [a typical Johannine double-
sense] from the earth". There are remains of copper mines
in the desert of the south of Israel, some forty kilometres
from Eilat, where I have myself picked up little squiggles

of smelted copper. Snakes are often known as objects of worship in primitive religions. The puzzle is that such worship is here mentioned without criticism, and as a precedent for the Passion of Jesus. Is this mention in the Book of Numbers simply an attempt to associate such squiggles, presumably well known in Israel, with Moses and the wanderings of Israel?

The Gospel reading is rendered more mysterious and suggestive by the Johannine ambiguity and contrast. One scholar remarked that John "has duality in his bones": above and below, sons of light and sons of darkness, truth and falsehood, light and darkness, life and death, blind and sighted. The same is true of ambiguity. What does "lifted up from the earth" mean? Or "exalted"? Is it a reference to Jesus' position on the cross, or a statement of his exaltation to heaven? What does Jesus mean by "going away"? What did he mean by "living bread", "living water"? In John there are often several levels of meaning. This is all part of showing that Jesus is mysterious and unfathomable, and cannot be fully comprehended by normal human terms.

The most mysterious and at the same time pregnant claim is "I am he", which comes twice in this passage. This may be interpreted as a claim to the divine name itself, for "I am he" or "I am" is the name which was revealed to Moses at the Burning Bush (*Ex* 3:14). Jesus makes the claim several times, ever more clearly. This expression has three possible levels of meaning. It can be no more than a self-identification: "Don't be afraid. It is me", as when Jesus comes walking on the Lake (6:20). It can be made with a predicate ("I am the living bread", "I am the light of the world"). But without a predicate it becomes clearer and clearer that it has a special meaning, until at last (8:58) they realise that Jesus is claiming the divine Name itself, and start to throw stones at him for blasphemy.

Action:

Am I really honest with myself about what God is trying to say to me, or do I block out what God is asking if it happens to be inconvenient?

Wednesday

> *Jesus answered:*
> *"If God were your father, you would love me,*
> *since I have come here from God; yes,*
> *I have come from him;*
> *not that I came because I chose,*
> *no, I was sent, and by him."*
>
> Dn 3:14-20, 24-25, 28; Jn 8:31-42

✠

The threat of violence is coming closer, and the first reading, about the Three Young Men in the Fiery Furnace, prepares us by giving a precedent. Fidelity to the commands of God brings its own dangers in any age. The fictional story of the Three Young Men - here given in a sharply abbreviated form - is set at the court of Babylon. The three had been prepared for their ordeal by their fidelity to the Law from their youth. Martyrdom does not arise all of a sudden, but is prepared by a life of faithful devotion.

The Gospel passage continues the confrontation of Jesus with "the Jews" in the Temple. The argument now centres on fidelity to Abraham as the founder of the Hebrew and Jewish tradition of Law. Mere physical descent from Abraham is of no avail; Jesus is here preparing for the advent of gentiles into the salvation promised to the Jews. This is prepared also by the synoptic tradition: the Baptist taught that God could raise up children for Abraham from the stones (*Mt* 3:7-10), and on other occasions a warning was given that gentiles would take the place of the children of Abraham at the heavenly banquet (*Mt* 8:11-12). We now have the paradox that "salvation comes from the Jews" (*Jn* 4:22), but the Jews refused to receive it for themselves. So Jesus can accuse his interlocutors, "the devil is your father", not Abraham.

There are also two unusual features. The first is that normally Abraham is the figure of faith: this is where all the stress comes in Paul, particularly in Romans 4, which is a long meditation on the faith of Abraham, which was considered as justifying him. It was the faith of Abraham in responding to God's call to go out into the desert with no normal, human hope or guarantee that brought him salvation.

The second unusual feature is that salvation seems to consist in obeying the Law, whereas in John it is usually uniquely in love, sharing in the mutual love of Father and Son, rather than observance of Law. At the end of this passage we are reminded of the obedient love of Jesus for his Father. In the course of the discourses after the Last Supper this will become more and more the dominant motif. Christians must love one another with the same love of utter self-sacrifice which Jesus is about to show by his love for the Father in his Passion. In the Greek tradition there was little conception of this love. It is not the love of mere friendship (*philia*) nor sexual attraction (*eros*). To express the Hebrew concept of family love which puts no limit on the self-sacrifice implied a little-used word (*agape*) is adopted and filled with new meaning. It is the love of a mother who cannot forget the baby at her breast.

Action:

For the remainder of Lent perhaps make a special effort to show Christian love, courtesy and even affection for someone whom one tends to dislike or avoid.

Thursday

*The Jews then said, "You are not fifty yet,
and you have seen Abraham!"*

Jesus replied:

*"I tell you most solemnly,
before Abraham ever was,
I Am."*

Gn 17:3-9; Jn 8:51-59

✠

God's eternal covenant with Abraham was the basis of the confidence of the Israelites. However much they sinned, God would never withdraw this covenant. Even when all seemed lost at the time of the Exile, the promise of a renewed covenant, greater than the old covenant because it was a personal covenant, was given. But in each of the three accounts of the covenant with Abraham there is mention of the other nations. The covenant was never exclusively for the Jews, even though this dimension is only touched, not emphasised, in the early tradition. It must be remembered that these passages of Genesis were finally edited only after the return from Babylon, when the Jews were becoming more acutely conscious that other nations were to come and draw salvation from Jerusalem.

The Gospel passage continues the account, read on the last two days, of the confrontation of Jesus with "the Jews" in the Temple at the Festival of Tabernacles. With that mysterious ambiguity which is such a feature of the Gospel of John Jesus suggests his own eternity - and that in three ways: Abraham saw his Day, he adopts as his own the divine Name, 'I am' (see p.109), and he claims glory conferred by the Father.

This concept of glory (*doxa*), which the Father confers on Jesus, is awesome and inspiring. It is properly a divine property. In secular language it means glory, human renown or reputation, (*Jn* 5:41) something on which someone might preen himself or herself. But with the Johannine convention of deeper levels of meaning it indicates far more. When Moses, despairing at the failure of the Israelites immediately after the conclusion of the Covenant on Sinai, asks to see God's glory (*Ex* 33:8); he sees God's glory only from behind, for no one can see God and live. Then again Isaiah, in his vision in the Temple, is bowled over by the sight of God's glory (*Is* 6), and again Ezekiel is bowled over by seeing something that "looked like the glory of the Lord" (*Ezk* 1:28). So glory properly belongs to God alone, and is a terrifying and awesome sight. In the Prologue to John's Gospel "we saw his glory" is the summit of revelation at the Incarnation. By his first sign at Cana Jesus made his glory known (2:11), but the fullness of his glory is to be shown only by the Hour of his Passion and Resurrection, the two being seen as one single moment: "Now, Father, it is time for you to glorify me with that glory I had with you before the world was" (17:5). So the revelation of God's glory in Jesus is another way of expressing the divinity of Christ.

Action:

Meditate a little on the daunting glory of God, revealed in Jesus Christ. Perhaps read and appreciate the biblical passages here cited.

Friday

Yet you say to someone the Father has consecrated and
* sent into the world,*
* "You are blaspheming,"*
because he says, "I am the Son of God."
If I am not doing my Father's work,
there is no need to believe me.

Jr 20:10-13; Jn 10:31-42

✠

As the pressure on Jesus increases, the Church gives us for the first reading another passage of Jeremiah where the prophet expresses his unshakable faith in the divine protection. From his first vocation vision onwards he had protested against his enforced task of proclaiming the bad news of the impending fall of Jerusalem. One of the consequences which hit him hardest seems to have been the loss of his friends. Here he is announcing the danger in which he finds himself if he should put a foot wrong, but at the same time his confident praise of the Lord for protecting him through thick and thin. Jesus is in much the same situation.

In this further scene of confrontation between Jesus and his opponents we have moved to another festival, that of the Dedication. This is consonant with John's theme that Jesus takes over, or centres in himself, all the festivals of Judaism: he has taken over the Sabbath by (like God) working on the Sabbath. He has taken over the Festival of Tabernacles by claiming that he is the source of the living water which was a part of the ritual of the festival. He will take over the Passover by making it his own Festival of the New Covenant. So now he takes over the Festival of the Dedication, saying that he is the one who was truly consecrated by the Father, not the Temple whose re-dedication was being celebrated.

Jesus here also uses a neat rabbinical argument, one of the processes of interpretation codified by Rabbi Hillel (see p.75), the argument *a minori ad majus*, "from the lesser to the greater": if it was legitimate to call judges "gods" because by judging they are exercising the function of God, then it was even more legitimate to call "God" him who is rightly so called, namely Jesus.

There is an interesting parallel between these scenes in John of final controversy and the synoptic account of the hearing before the Jewish authorities. In Matthew and Mark the crunch point is the question put by the High Priest whether Jesus is "son of the Blessed One" (*Mk* 14:62). This is also the final question in the slightly different Lukan version (*Lk* 22:70-71). In both versions Jesus is accused of blasphemy for accepting the title of

"Son of God". Similarly in the Johannine account of the final controversies Jesus is accused of calling himself "Son of God" and claiming the divine title, and is charged with blasphemy for so doing. It may be that the synoptic account condenses into the one scene of the hearing elements which occur more diffused in the Johannine controversies. In either case the evangelists are telling us that the crunch point of the accusations against Jesus, the real reason for his condemnation, is his claim to be divine. It is not a matter of legal disputes, not yet of the disturbance in the Temple.

Action:

Am I ever responsible for making false accusations about anyone, or indeed of spreading damaging and possibly true gossip?

Saturday

> *One of them, Caiaphas, the high priest that year, said,*
> *"You don't seem to have grasped the situation at all;*
> *you fail to see that it is better for one man to die for*
> *the people, than for the whole nation to be destroyed."*
> *He did not speak in his own person, it was as high*
> *priest that he made this prophecy that Jesus was to die*
> *for the nation.*
>
> *Ezk 37:21-28; Jn 11:45-56*

✠

The two readings for today both prepare for Palm Sunday, the Sunday of the Passion, but in different ways, by prophecy and by history. The first reading, spoken by Ezekiel in the Babylonian Exile, is a promise of forgiveness and return, a renewal of the covenant which Israel had so determinedly broken by its idolatry and by its betrayal, turning to alliance with other nations and their gods, rather than trusting in the Lord. It is one of the few passages in exilic and post-exilic prophecy where David is prominent in the expectation. Before the disaster of the Exile the promises of God to David had been in the centre of Judah's hopes. However, at the fall of Jerusalem these promises seemed to have run into the sand and quietly disappeared.

Now, in this chapter and in Ezekiel 34, there is a revival of the Davidic hope: God will send a new David as a new ruler and shepherd. But at the same time the promise is that God himself will come to shepherd Israel: "I myself will pasture my sheep, I shall look for the lost one, bring back the stray. I shall be a true shepherd to them" (*Ezk* 34:15-16). Is David to be the shepherd or God himself? Is this new David to be God's representative or God himself? It seems that the promise will be accomplished by God himself fulfilling the role of David; there is a sort of shimmering between the two. For us, after the event, and believing that in Jesus God himself became incarnate as the new David, the matter is clearer. In the prophecy it is no more than hinted.

The Gospel reading takes us back to the aftermath of last Sunday's Gospel, the raising of Lazarus. It is typical of John's contrasts that the gift of life to Lazarus brings death to Jesus: it is in reaction to the crowds going out to see the renewed Lazarus (Bethany is twenty minutes' walk from Jerusalem) that the High Priest holds his meeting. The Johannine account of the Passion has no meeting of the Jewish authorities after the arrest of Jesus (only the personal meeting of Jesus with Annas); today's reading suggests an alternative chronology, that the decisive meeting took place well before the arrest. There would then have been no need for a crisis meeting of the High Priest and his advisors after the arrest of Jesus.

The crux of this meeting is Caiaphas's unconscious prophecy. He says more than he realises; it is another case of the many levels at which sayings in John can be understood; the Christian understands it on a quite different level than that intended by the speaker. It has uncanny echoes, as though the High Priest were making his own Jesus' saying, "The Son of Man came not to be served but to serve, and give his life as a ransom for many".

Action:

What can I do to give life to someone, to improve someone's quality of life - either long-term or at least to bring a few moments of joy?

Passion Sunday

> *... taking the form of a servant,*
> *born in human likeness, and found in human shape;*
> *he humbled himself,*
> *becoming obedient unto death, death on a cross.*
>
> *Is* 50:4-7; *Ph* 2:6-11

☩

The Gospel reading at the Eucharist itself is the Passion narrative according to Matthew, commented elsewhere. This leaves open the opportunity for a more extensive consideration of the reading from Paul's Letter to the Philippians.

A most attractive theory is that Paul did not himself compose the hymn, but adopted it, slightly altered it and included it. The balance and rhythm are not characteristic of Paul's jerky, excitable style. We know from a letter of Pliny, governor of the Roman province of Bithynia in ad 114, that a chief element in the Christian worship was to meet "on a set day" (presumably Sunday) and to sing a hymn "to Christ as to a God". This could be just such a hymn, in three four-line stanzas.

Being in the form of God,

He did not count equality with God

something to be grasped.

But he emptied himself

The basic thought of this first stanza is a contrast with Adam. Adam was made in the image of God (a different word from the *form* of God), but he thought that equality with God was something to be grasped. The Greek word here for 'grasped' implies snatching, grabbing, taking for oneself and treasuring, possibly unfairly. The first Adam wanted to be like God and escape death; the Second Adam took the opposite route and emptied himself.

taking the form of a servant,

born in human likeness, and found in human shape;

he humbled himself,

becoming obedient unto death, death on a cross.

The first line of this second stanza contrasts with the first line of the first: each beings with a participle and "the form of" God and man respectively. The word translated "servant" may mean "slave", but more probably it is a reference to the Songs of the Suffering Servant of the Lord: it echoes Jesus' words, he came "not to be served but to serve". Possibly the final phrase, "death on a cross", which somewhat spoils the rhythm, was added by Paul to express his constant emphasis on the saving value of the cross.

And therefore God highly exalted him,

and granted him the name above every name

so that at the name of Jesus

Every knee should bend and every tongue acknowledge
   that Jesus Christ is Lord,

to the glory of God the Father.

In the final stanza, in a staggering reversal, Paul attributes to Jesus the name "Lord", which is the sacred Name of God in the Hebrew Bible. Not only that, but the hymn gives to Jesus the strongly monotheist homage due to the Lord alone in Isaiah 45:23. Far from being a blasphemy, this is, on the contrary, "to the glory of God the Father" - an extra line, perhaps added by Paul.

Action:

Spend some time praying in thanksgiving and wonder.

Monday

Leave her alone; she had to keep this scent for the day
of my burial. You have the poor with you always,
you will not always have me.

Is 42:1-7; Jn 12:1-11

✠

Today we begin reading the Songs of the Servant in Isaiah.
These four songs, read in succession as the first readings
during Holy Week, hang together. They depict a servant
of the Lord, wholly dedicated to the Lord, and pleasing to
him, who will bring true justice to Israel and to the nations,
and will suffer hideously and die in the Lord's service,
and will eventually be justified. Is the prophet speaking
of himself, of the nation of Israel or of some particular
individual among Israel? Whatever the original meaning,
Christian tradition has applied these songs to Jesus and
his mission. Not without good reason, for the Voice
from heaven to Jesus at the Baptism is at least alluding
to Jesus with this opening of the first song, "Here is my
servant whom I uphold, my chosen one in whom my soul
delights". Following on from this, Jesus speaks frequently
of his mission of service, "the Son of Man came not to be
served but to serve", and of the duty of his followers to

serve in the same way. It could, therefore, be the whole clue to Jesus' mission and proclamation, as he is "the light of the nations, to open the eyes of the blind".

As it is six days before the Passover (counting inclusively), the Gospel reading is appropriately the story of the anointing of Jesus' feet with costly ointment at Bethany. In Mark and Matthew the woman is unnamed, but John names her as Mary, sister of Martha and Lazarus. John is more familiar with Jerusalem and its environs than are the synoptics, and may have the family as his source. The response of Jesus to her act of loving, personal devotion and his rebuke to the eminently practical objection of Judas, raise the question repeatedly asked of the Church (and never definitively settled), how much money should be spent on gifts to adorn churches and their liturgy, and how much given to the poor and needy. How much did Jesus know of the future? His answer shows his awareness of the increasing tension.

Why did Judas betray his Master? Was it simply for thirty pieces of silver, or is his greed a subsequent development? It is not mentioned by the synoptic Gospels. Was it a goodwill gesture which went wrong? It has been suggested that he merely wanted to bring Jesus together with the High Priest. Was Judas a convinced nationalist fighter (his name is nationalist) who abandoned Jesus in frustration when he perceived that Jesus' concept of messiahship did not include expulsion of the Romans?

Action:

A gift - but should it be to the living stones of the Church or to the edifice? Either would be appropriate to the end of Lent and Holy Week.

Tuesday

"Lay down your life for me?" answered Jesus. "I tell you most solemnly, before the cock crows you will have disowned me three times."

Is 49:1-6; Jn 13:21-33, 36-38

✠

In this second Song of the Servant the stress is upon the mission of the servant for the nations. Here the Servant is named "Israel" (though some think this name is an addition), and his task is not merely to bring back the survivors of Israel, but also to be the light to the nations, a phrase picked up in Simeon's canticle. These Songs find their place in the central section of Isaiah, written during the Exile at Babylon, when Israel was beginning to be aware that the vocation of Israel was to bring salvation to other nations of the world. On the other hand, the two mentions of "born from my mother's womb", "formed in the womb" do suggest that it is the song of an individual. Perhaps it is an individual representing Israel, just as Jesus is the focal point, in whom all the hopes of Israel find their realisation.

The Gospel reading jumps a little ahead, to the Last Supper. Rather than telling us the story of the Last Supper, the Gospels give us only two incidents at the Supper, the marking of the traitor and the Institution of the Eucharist. The latter is absent from John, who reserves the sacraments till after the death of Jesus and the foundation of the Church. John identifies the traitor, but the synoptic Gospels stress not his identity, but his treachery, the one who dips his hand in the dish with Jesus and immediately betrays this gesture of fellowship. In our readings we have the betrayal on Tuesday (John) and Wednesday (Matthew), while the Eucharist is reserved for Thursday.

The Church puts before us the failure of the disciples, or rather the failure of the whole body of disciples, led by Peter. Throughout Jesus' ministry this has been a theme, especially in Mark. Three times the disciples are rebuked for their failure to understand who Jesus is, each time on the Lake of Galilee, before - immediately after the gift of sight to the blind man of Bethsaida - Peter bursts out with his profession of faith, "You are the Christ/Messiah" (*Mk* 8:29). After this turning point of the Gospel, again three times they fail to grasp the teaching on suffering, that as Messiah Jesus can accomplish his mission only by suffering and death, and that his disciples must share this suffering. The theme reaches its climax with Peter's repeated protestation at the Supper that he is ready to die with Jesus, and his panicked denial when he is accosted by the diminutive servant girl outside the High Priest's house. In John at any rate we hear the story of his repentance and response to the Risen Christ's threefold challenge at the Lakeside. The prominence given to this theme is surely a reminder that the Twelve are role models for future disciples even in their failure - and in their repentance. Perfection is not required, only repentance.

Action:

The placing of this reminder of failure and betrayal by the closest companions of Jesus may be deliberate, to give us time to prepare for the Sacrament of Reconciliation.

Spy Wednesday

When evening came he was at table with the twelve
disciples. And while they were eating he said, "I tell you
solemnly, one of you is about to betray me."

Is 50:4-9; Mt 26:14-25

✠

In the third Song of the Servant, read today, the theme of
the Servant suffering insult and persecution, and the theme
of a legal trial begin to be voiced, though not as strongly
as in the fourth Song. Equally strong are the themes of the
obedience of the Servant and the Servant's confidence in
divine help.

The positioning of the Gospel passages is beginning
to get a little wobbly! The Church wishes us to hear the
important passages, but cannot fit them all onto the correct
days. The disciples are sent to make the preparations, surely
on the day when the Supper will be eaten in the evening.
There is an air of mystery about the preparations: both in
getting the donkey for Palm Sunday and in preparing the
room for the Passover Jesus sends two disciples into the
city with instructions about meeting an unknown man. That
both of these missions work out smoothly surely indicates
that Jesus has complete foreknowledge and control.

The situation is more complicated because the temporal inter-relationship of the Great Events and of the Passover is unclear. The Jewish day begins at sundown, so the Passover supper begins the Day of Passover. In the synoptic Gospels Jesus eats the Passover with his disciples the evening before he suffers, so that the Day of Passover should be the day of his death. In John the Jewish leaders refuse to enter Pilate's palace to avoid the uncleanness which will prevent them eating the Passover. Therefore according to John's timing Jesus' Last Supper occurs twenty four hours before the Passover supper and Jesus dies as the Passover lambs are being slaughtered just in time for the supper. There are sound theological reasons for each of these: the synoptics stress that the Last Supper is a Passover; John stresses that Jesus is the paschal lamb.

Throughout the life of Jesus, but especially in the narrative of the Passion, the fulfilment of Scripture is important. The most ancient tradition of the Church, seen in 1 Corinthians 15:3-5, was clear that Jesus died "according to the scriptures" and rose "according to the scriptures". This event, the "Hour" of Jesus was the climax of Israel's history, to which the whole thrust of the story was tending. Therefore it is stressed by many quotations from the scriptures that it was bound to be so. The thirty silver pieces for which Jesus was sold may be an allusion to Exodus 21:32, the compensation for a slave gored by an ox. Many details of the narrative may have their chief point in fulfilling just such a scriptural text.

Action:

Invite someone to a meal and take special trouble preparing it, as if it were being prepared for Christ himself.

Maundy Thursday

When he had washed their feet and put on his clothes
again he went back to the table. "Do you understand"
he said "what I have done to you? You call me Master
and Lord, and rightly; so I am. If I, then, the Lord and
Master, have washed your feet, you should wash each
other's feet."

Ex 12:1-8, 11-14; *1 Co* 11:23-26; *Jn* 13:1-15

✠

The festival on which Passover was based was originally
a nomad festival at the move from winter pastures in the
plains to summer pastures in the hills. A fine lamb was
offered to placate the gods, so that they would not harm
the rest of the flock; it was eaten at the first full moon of
spring, after the spring equinox (21st March). Blood on
the doorposts of the tents was a sign that the offering had
been made. Water is scarce for nomads, so the lamb was
roasted, not boiled - cooking pots were packed, anyway!
This primitive festival was taken up by the Hebrews to
commemorate the great move from Egypt through the
desert, and - most of all - the covenant made in the desert
of Sinai, when God made Israel his own people. It was
celebrated each year, and the blood of the lamb sprinkled

over the altar (representing God) and the people signified their union in the covenant.

This feast was taken up by Jesus as the occasion for him to make his own new covenant, fulfilling the promises made by the prophets of a new covenant to replace the old covenant so definitively broken at the time of the Babylonian Exile. Whether Jesus celebrated it on the traditional evening or the day before is unclear (see yesterday's discussion); if it was not the conventional day he must have taken this last opportunity to make it his own Passover Festival with his community. Paul gives us the story of this meal, which he himself had received from what was already traditional, hardly a dozen years after the Last Supper, well before the Gospels were written. Jesus himself was the lamb who was to be sacrificed, and his new covenant was sealed, not in blood sprinkled, but in his own blood consumed. It was a 'memorial', that is, an effective re-enactment, actually renewing the act of dedication and union. In today's reading Paul is rebuking the Corinthians for re-enacting this significant moment thoughtlessly, as though it was an ordinary festal meal; they had lost the intention and the seriousness. They were no longer proclaiming the death of Jesus, no longer engaging themselves in the new covenant. It is a dangerous thing to commit oneself to a new covenant sealed by death and leading to new life.

Jesus' extraordinary gesture recorded in the Gospel of John shows us the full meaning of what he was doing. The narrative stresses that Jesus knew what was to come; he was showing his disciples the meaning of the events. By the act of rising from the table and performing the demeaning act of stripping down and washing the feet of his followers, his guests, he was showing the meaning of the dire events to come - Peter's horror says it all, but there was far worse to come. It was a pre-enactment of his great act of serving his community, the new family which he was binding to himself by this new covenant, the foundational act of service in the Church.

Action

What act of service can I perform for the sake of the community of Christ's family in which I live?

Good Friday

"After Jesus had taken the vinegar he said, 'It is accomplished'; and bowing his head he gave up the spirit."

Is 52:13-53:12; *Heb* 4:14-16; 5:7-9; *Jn* 18:1-19:42

✠

John's narrative of the Passion is different from that of the synoptic Gospels in important respects. Some of these differences are matters of emphasis, others spring from a set of different facts. After Caiaphas's decision (see p.119) no Jewish trial scene before the High Priest, no meeting of a Sanhedrin to prepare a charge to put before Pilate, was necessary. Instead John gives an interrogation before Annas, the ex-High Priest and father-in-law of Caiaphas. The trial before Pilate may well be built on the same incident as that of the synoptics, but in John it is highly elaborated for theological reasons.

The Johannine account is not the story of a condemned criminal being dragged to the disgraceful and tortured death reserved for slaves. Jesus is the majestic king, who proceeds royally to his triumph in death. There is no painful prayer for release in Gethsemane. From the beginning it is stressed that Jesus is fully aware of what is to happen. Before he can be arrested his captors repeatedly fall to the ground in an involuntary gesture of reverence at Jesus' pronouncement of the divine name, "I am". Jesus commands them to let his followers go, and is taken only when he gives the word (18:11). The humiliating elements of the other accounts, such as buffeting, spitting and the challenge to prophesy, have disappeared. Jesus is emphatically declared king in the three great world languages by the very man who condemns him to death (19:20-22). John even notes that the proclamation was publicly acknowledged by "many of the Jews".

Not only is Jesus king; he continues his role as revealer and judge as well. In the interview with Annas it is Jesus who challenges and questions the High Priest, reiterating his own teaching which he has given for all the world to hear. Similarly at the trial before Pilate, Jesus questions the governor and shows his control, until Pilate collapses with the feeble evasion, "What is truth?" - a humiliating self-condemnation in this gospel of truth. The judgement reaches its climax when the Jewish leaders, in a formal and balanced scene, condemn themselves before Jesus: he is enthroned on the judgement seat as judge and crowned - with thorns - as king, still wearing the royal purple robe of his mockery, while they deny the very existence of Judaism by declaring, "We have no king but Caesar" (19:15). If the God of Israel is not universal king, then Israel has no point or purpose.

The final scene has special significance. Jesus carries his own cross, unaided, and is enthroned on it - no agonising details of nailing and hoisting - between two attendants. There is no final psalm quotation of seeming despair (as in Mark and Matthew) or of resignation (as in Luke), no wordless "great cry" as Jesus expires. In John Jesus prepares the community of the future. In contrast to the other Gospels, Mary and the Beloved Disciple stand at the foot of the cross and are entrusted to each other's care to constitute the first Christian community, the woman and the man, the mother and the ideal disciple. This is cemented by the gift of the Spirit, as Jesus - with typical Johannine ambiguity - "gave over his spirit". Does this mean "breathed his last" or "gave them the Holy Spirit"? Only then does Jesus consent to die, with the words, "It is fulfilled".

Action:

Spend some time reflecting on the death of Jesus.
What is its most significant aspect for you?

Holy Saturday

There is no liturgy on this day. The Church awaits the celebration of the triumph of the Resurrection at the Easter Vigil and on the day of Resurrection itself.

Easter Sunday

*...get rid of all the old yeast, and make yourselves
into a completely new batch of bread, unleavened as
you are meant to be. Christ, our Passover, has been
sacrificed; let us celebrate the feast, by getting rid
of all the old yeast of evil and wickedness, having only
the unleavened bread of sincerity and truth.*

Ac 10:34, 37-43; Col 3:1-4 or 1 Co 5:6-8; Jn 20:1-9

✠

It is not the empty tomb which is the focus of Easter; that
is merely a negative finding, the body of Jesus is no longer
there. What is important - and is stressed particularly by
the first two readings - is what has happened to Jesus, to
the Risen Christ. The first reading from the speech of Peter
to the crowds at Pentecost tells us that God has raised him
to be the Judge of the living and the dead - as in Matthew's
scene of the last judgement when Christ, enthroned and
surrounded by his angels, separates sheep from goats. The
same is stressed by the reading from Colossians, "where
Christ is, sitting at God's right hand". This is the claim of
Jesus at the hearing before the High Priest, "you will see
the Son of Man seated at the right hand of the Power and
coming on the clouds of heaven." It is the claim in the words
of the Psalm, "the Lord said to my Lord, 'Sit at my right

hand'", a claim that the Risen Christ is to share the throne of God, an incredible claim for a human being, causing the High Priest to tear his robe in horror at the blasphemy. No human words can describe what this means, for we have no experience of it from which we could form the words or images. We can only say what it is not. It is transcendent, that is, beyond all human experience. It cannot be put into human language, as Paul says in his reference to being 'caught up into Paradise' (*2 Co* 12:4). Paul says it is silly to ask what sort of body it is.

Jesus did not come back to life; he went forward to life, a new kind of life which we are too limited in mind even to envisage. All Paul can say is that it is a transformation: "we shall not all die, but we shall all be changed" after the model of the Risen Christ. As with the Risen Christ, so with ourselves, there is continuity but transformation. We shall be permeated with God, strong with the strength of God, imperishable with the imperishability of God, filled with the glory of God. The animating principle is no longer the human soul, but is the Spirit of God (*1 Co* 15:42-44). Whatever happens, both Peter and Paul are transfixed with joy at the idea.

In the alternative second reading from 1 Corinthians Paul puts it in terms of the Passover yeast, the new leaven which makes the loaf rise. This is again an image of novelty and wondrous, 'inexplicable' transformation. But it does show that in our Easter joy we should reject all the tired, soiled and corrupt yeast of our previous existence, and go forward to a new way of life.

Action:

In the Eastern Churches during the Easter season everyone goes around with the greeting, "Christ is risen", to which the answer is "He is truly risen". Let us try that greeting, at least in our hearts, to all we meet!